OLD WORLD PSYCHIC MEDIUM

GREG NICHOLAS

with

KAT RODGERS

DEDICATION

To God for my Gifts and abilities to communicate with the Spirit World for the highest and best good. And for His presence at each mediumistic communication.

To my Late mother and grandmothers for passing down their knowledge, encouragement, and support of their old world ways of mediumship. People need to hear what God has to say.

To my Late father for his genuine love and contribution of good genes and DNA. But, did I really have to inherit my bald head from you?

Acknowledgments

To my brother, John, and my loving wife, Jan, for standing beside me.

To Kat Rodgers for her belief in me–I am forever grateful.

To my clients who trust me and receive benefit.

To the Spirits who help and guide me.

You all inspire me to do God's work. Without you, this book would not have been written to plant seeds of awareness for others.

Cover Photo

Monte Cassino Abbey, situated atop the awe-inspiring Sibylline Mountain in Italy, stands in the background of The Monastery of Saint Benedict. Gregory Nicholas' bloodline of maternal descendants originated near there in Naples where his great-grandmother, Maria, lived.

Maria, known as the good 'white witch,' would frequently travel there and climb that steep slope for prayer and meditation. She kept to herself but privately used her misunderstood psychic medium abilities for good intent and purpose. Individuals sought her out for any situation such as removing evil spells, hexes, and personal torment.

After her daughter, Elizabeth, lost a husband in World War I, they immigrated to America with Maria's first two grandchildren on the SS Providence. Her God-honored abilities were passed down over four generations.

BORN INTO PSYCHIC MEDIUMS

I am the fourth generation of natural born psychic mediums who descended from my great-grandmother from Italy. Unlike my ancestors, I was fortunately the first in our family, at liberty, to openly use our God-given abilities. It wasn't until my generation that society finally began to accept the practice and demonstrations by psychic mediums.

On Saint Patrick's Day of 1962, I was born in Oil City, PA. Remarkably, the doctor and my mother knew I was blessed with 'The Gift' the moment I crowned. I was born en caul. My face was draped with 'the veil', a rarity. The amniotic sac completely caressed my face and head in a soft jello-like bubble. According to Grandma Elizabeth, a veiled birth was a good luck sign. In her eyes, heart, and faith, she considered me a miracle baby from God, not just an 'accident.'

John, my only sibling, is thirteen years older than I. He's the polar opposite of me—quiet, reserved, intelligent, great with numbers, and a corporate executive in Rochester, New York. When Mom was seven months pregnant with him, she fell down a flight of steps. The doctor said she would never be able to have more children due to her injuries. Thirteen years later, God said differently. For the first four months of Mom's pregnancy, everyone thought she was having a gallbladder problem. Everyone was surprised to discover she was pregnant again. I agree with my grandmother; I was no accident!

Religion forever shadowed my birthday. The Catholic church recognized March 17th as a feast day commemorating Ireland's most beloved patron saint, Saint Patrick. And, with rare exception, this date usually falls during the Christian holy season of Lent.

I was the only grandson to inherit the blood lines of mediumship from our great-grandmother, Maria, from Naples, Italy. This woman once lived in a small village of Belone, living in a home with dirt floors. She saw an opportunity to immigrate to the United States in 1919 on the SS Providence with a child, Elizabeth. Her first husband had died in Italy during World War I. Three weeks after she arrived, Grandma Elizabeth met my grandfather, Macario, who owned a farm in Oil City, where she married him and settled.

I never met my great-grandmother, Maria, for she passed in the early 1930's before I was born. Her memory lived on through her daughter—my grandmother, Elizabeth, and on through her daughter—my mother, Rose.

My favorite memories of Grandma Elizabeth were the Italian lullabies she sang to me. She taught me them with hopes that one day I'd sing them to my own kids. Ironically, who would have known that I'd marry and not be able to conceive children nor have the opportunity to continue the lineal decent of our bloodline.

Spiritual "Gifts" were inherited through our maternal side of the family. One female in each generation was born a psychic medium. This means we are able to feel and hear thoughts, voices, or mental impressions from the Spirit World. Many mediums can see spirits as they speak. It is known as the practice called 'mediumship.' This is when a medium, like myself, has an ability to connect and communicate with a spirit-person and convey what they say in what is called a 'reading.'

MY FIRST AWARENESS OF SPIRIT

My first recollection of "seeing things" began around the age of four. At that young age, I recall being all dressed up with my family. We attended a funeral. As I stood beside my mother in the funeral parlor, I saw what looked like a transparent human figure, walking around in a dress—an identical twin to the woman in the casket. It intrigued me. There was no association with feeling afraid.

I tugged at my mother's arm and pointed. "Mommy, there's that same lady standing over there."

"We'll talk about it later," she replied.

Later, Mom explained that the lady I saw was a spirit of the woman who laid in the casket. I accepted it as a normal part of life and death, which stuck with me throughout life. Then, when I turned ten years old, I witnessed the same thing when Grandma Elizabeth passed of senility, our modern day Alzheimer's disease.

In our family, there were many traditions and customs we adhered to. I was fascinated and observant of them as I grew up. Mom always sent bouquets of red flowers for funerals as a sign of love. If death happened at home, the body was carried out feet first so it wouldn't return to the residence.

Mom always made sure that none of us wore purple to funerals. We were not worthy to wear that color because Christ dressed in a purple robe. It was once an expensive color exclusively reserved for royalty. Our clothes were black, a dye for mourning those who die. That strict family custom ceased about fifty years ago but some relatives preferred to abide by it.

At the funeral home, before the public viewing of Grandma Elizabeth, Aunt Mary gave me pink, fuzzy slippers to dress Grandma's feet. It was customary to always put shoes, socks, or slippers on the dead to make sure they got into Heaven. Being short in stature, I stood on the kneeler which was positioned front and center of the casket. Graciously and respectfully, I reached over and turned up the blanket that lay across her legs and feet. I wiggled on her slippers and said, "Now you're buried in pink, Grandma."

I could 'see' with my spiritual eyes that my grandmother had joined her husband, Macario, in Heaven. Even though he had passed five days before my first birthday, I 'knew' who he was.

During our turn at the casket, we always touched the dead one's hand so they would protect us, and for good dreams. We would kiss or touch the body as a final act of respect. Devout Catholics would kneel on the kneeler in front of the casket and pray the rosary.

In those days, a funeral wake was usually held at a funeral home for two or three days of calling hours to view the body and pay respects. My family would sit and pray the rosary for an entire 45 minutes before a short service began each day.

Afterwards, a few friends, neighbors, and family would stop by the deceased loved one's home to visit, eat, or drop off homemade food. Small gatherings happened every evening until the body was laid to rest. On the day of the funeral, everyone in attendance got invited to the big funeral dinner. It was a catered affair that allowed the family and guests time to celebrate the life and memories of that special person.

I vividly remember my childhood, when on occasions, the viewings were conducted in the home of the onc who crossed over. Family members would stay up all night to keep a watch over the body. That was done to ensure protection for the spirit of the deceased loved one until the funeral when they were given over to God's hands. Also, it was done as a sign of respect and a way to pay back the deceased for everything they had done while alive.

MY FAVORITE CHILDHOOD STORIES

Bible stories serve a purpose to teach people of all ages and walks of life about God. They instill concepts and an understanding of what He is like as a loving, invisible Being. Stories offer inspiration and application in our daily lives and uplift us in between the weight of the Scripture, genealogies, and laws. As a child, the relatable stories I learned from the Holy Book were key to the development of my passion to hold my "Gift" from God in highest reverence to honor, obey, and serve in helping others know about Him. The following abbreviated versions are my childhood favorites:

DANIEL AND THE LION'S DEN

The Biblical story "Daniel In The Lion's Den" tells how jealous rivals tricked Daniel to issue a decree designed to condemn him to death. King Darius ordered Daniel to be thrown into a den of hungry lions....

At the break of dawn the following day, the king rushed to the lion's den and shouted. "Daniel, servant of the living God, has your God, whom you serve continually, been able to rescue you from the lions?"

"May the king live forever!" Daniel answered. "My God sent His angel, and He shut the mouths of the ferocious lions...."

In response, King Darius issued a decree to the world. In it, he praised God. "He rescues and He saves; He performs signs and wonders in the heavens and on earth. He has rescued Daniel from the lions."

Archangel Gabriel Visits Mary

The Christmas story began with an angel's visit to Earth. In the Bible, the encounter between the Archangel Gabriel and Mary, known as the annunciation, happened when God's archangel of revelation announced to a faithful teen virgin, Mary, that God had intentionally chosen her to give birth to a baby, named Jesus Christ. He was destined to save the world and Mary would become the mother of the world's Savior.

Jesus would be the head of a kingdom that would never end and be known as the Messiah that the Jewish people awaited. He was the one who would save people worldwide from sin and connect them to God for eternity. (Luke 1: 26-38)

The Three Kings

Discovering that the Messiah was to be born, three kings–Gaspar, Melchior, and Balthazar–organized an expedition to find Him. They immediately mounted camels and followed a special star that led them to Bethlehem and the baby Jesus. They took gifts to the newborn that symbolized the child's true identity and purpose: gold for a king, frankincense for God, and myrrh to be used to anoint the dead.

These wealthy kings, also known as magi or wise men, were also known as astrologers, seers, and fortunetellers. God honored these three travelers by warning them in a dream to return home by another route and to not report back to King Herod. They obeyed.

Some Bible scholars think Joseph and Mary sold the wise men's gifts to pay for their trip to Egypt to escape Herod's announcement to persecute all newborn males under age two years of age. The

Gospel of John states that Nicodemus brought a mixture of aloe and myrrh to anoint Jesus' body after the crucifixion. The gift of myrrh and frankincense, once priceless, was used in burial rituals as an embalming agent and to cover the odor of a dead body. As a child, I thought it was such an odd thing to give a newborn. My mother had said that it suggested their work as God's prophets and of the forthcoming crucifixion.

La Befana

During the Christmas season, I always put out my La Befana figurine, Italy's Christmas Witch. Some refer to her as 'the witch' or 'La Strega', in Italian. When I was young, it was our Italian tradition to spend the evening of each fifth of January in anticipation of her arrival. The next morning, my brother and I would be excited to find candies and small gifts she had left for us.

Italy celebrated January sixth for two reasons. It was the day, known as the Epiphany, when the three kings got to the crib of baby Jesus bearing gifts. Also, it was a celebration of La Befana—a hard-working, good-hearted, old, wrinkly, skinny witch with a big curved nose who dressed in layers of rags for warmth.

The traditional story of her began long ago on one fifth of January when the three kings stopped by while La Befana was at home broom-sweeping the floors. They invited her to go with them to see the new baby. She declined. The kings left.

She soon had a feeling that she should have accepted their invitation. They hadn't given details but she realized that there must be something about this child that was of more importance than a clean house. She decided that she would get there by herself and quickly packed up lots of presents to take along. Anxious to catch up with the kings, La Befana jumped on her magic broomstick and took off into the sky without even knowing which direction to go. She didn't know that the special star held the secret.

As the witch traveled, she stopped at homes along the way and hoped to find the baby or magi; but never found them. But, she did lightened her load each time she left behind gifts, goodies, and a chunk of coal to surprise the children when they woke up the following morning.

As the story goes, La Befana used her broomstick to fly as well as to sweep away any floor dirt or troubles. She always left everyone a clean slate on which to begin another new year.

Bible stories are real as well as symbolic. Actual people who lived during that time witnessed and confirmed prophecies about Jesus as truth and their written accounts hold symbolic meaning for eternity. They serve to show that Jesus came to save individuals, rich or poor, educated or not, from anywhere in the world. It all boils down to God's unconditional love for, and interaction with, the human race.

I have always related my biblical teachings to my 'calling.' My foundation in Biblical stories inspired me along my journey as did Mom's strong devotion to them and to the Blessed Mother. One of her favorite stories was introduced to me as a confused youngster when I questioned the title and meaning of an artwork entitled 'Our Lady of Lourdes.' Mom clarified that Lourdes wasn't an archaic spelling, or misspelling of 'lord's,' but a small town in France. She shared the story of a fourteen-year-old poor child, Bernadette Soubirous, who had experienced eighteen separate visions of a female apparition who claimed to be the 'Immaculate Conception' or 'Virgin Mary.' The lengthy story ended with Bernadette being canonized as a saint by the Catholic Church after much skepticism.

I identified with that story. I knew that I had been gifted special abilities from God to use for His purpose, but didn't exactly fully comprehend, as a teenager, what exactly that was until my father encouraged me, later, to 'get moving' in a dream. It was after that when I truly sensed a deeper appreciation and gratitude for all Mom's valuable time and formative teachings.

OUR TIES TO ASTROLOGY

When the 2020 Christmas holiday neared, "The Christmas Star" became the center of the world's attention and conversation. News channels, radio broadcasts, podcasts, friends, neighbors, and relatives seethed with excitement. Despite a pandemic, we were also in the midst of Advent—a season saturated in religious tradition, of retelling biblical stories such as the prophets' journey to deliver gifts to the newborn Jesus, led there by a single star. I caught threads of those stories being repeated as I flipped through television channels and listened to the radio. Memories of my mother reciting them each year to my brother and me cheered my soul.

I wondered how many people would discover God through shared biblical Christmas stories during the uptick in conversations about a similarity of a star that brilliantly sparkled in the late December's night sky. It became a source of inspiration as well as a brief distraction from the global pandemic. Joy and hope added much needed optimism as the death rate from COVID-19 spiked daily. Lockdowns, which ordered everyone to stay at home except for essential workers, remained in place to mitigate the spread of the deadly virus. The government urged everyone to wear masks, socially distance, wash hands, and use virtual media for work and socialization. Really? Would this virus ever end?

This occurrence brought hope and joy to many. Not only were stars a delight to view anytime, but people had a number of reasons to look forward to this phenomenon during the final month of 2020.

It was something that hadn't happened in this way for centuries. Interest and excitement heightened.

And, for many individuals who believed that these unique and rare occurrences of 'astronomical phenomena' were true signs which pointed to the 'Last Days,' or the second coming of Christ, this was their reminder to be vigilant of indications as directed in Revelation 8:12.

To me, in those darkest pandemic days, the stars seemed to reconnect full circle with meaningful evidence of God's connection to astrology. From my patio on December 21, 2020, I marveled at the most dazzling star I had ever seen. It mesmerized me. In that moment, I felt the incredible splendor of God's existence in that rare sight. Every cell in my body tingled in awe as it shined like a spiritual beacon against the dark clear sky.

It captivated me and stirred my imagination. My eyes beheld a likeness of that ancient star of David. I visualized the amazing wise men, astronomers of sorts, who were driven by blind faith, a strong belief in prophesy, and in one particular star as a true 'sign' of Jesus' birth to point their way to Bethlehem. I thought about Psalm 19:1. "The heavens declare the glory of God; the skies proclaim the work of His hand."

I stood in amazement and gazed at two of the largest planets in our solar system, Jupiter and Saturn, aligned so closely that they seemed to touch and form one super-duper luminous ball. They hadn't been positioned that close in 800 years, and predicted not to reoccur again until 2080. (1)

Chatter, discussions, and celestial observations extended beyond the end of the year into the 2021 New Year. People anticipated the arrival of January 5th to experience another unusual alignment of Jupiter, Mercury, and Saturn which created a triple planetary conjunction—in another seldom seen astrological event. (2)

I've always believed that Creation is divinely and harmoniously synchronized with astrology. From the beginning, God had designs on how to communicate with the world. Our heavenly bodies were created to show the world 'signs' of His intentions and guidance. They are part of human psyche and our ability to understand the totality of Creation through our intellectual interpretation of His messages.

His Spirit World uses astrology to send signs of spiritual communication to loved ones on earth through inspirational rainbows, shooting stars, meaningful cloud formations...and the northern lights interactions with individuals. Since childhood, I have been intrigued by astrology and other phenomena like 'The Christmas Star.'

HOW SPIRITUAL COMMUNICATION BEGAN: THE FOX FAMILY

The history of Spiritualism was taught by my mother's frequent storytelling. She repeated the stories often, as they were also favorites, verbally passed down over generations. One, in particular, about "the cabin and the Fox family," related to the first known communication with the Spirit World as evidenced by common, everyday phenomenon.

Once upon a historical time, a divine mystery began in a Hydesville cabin in New York State. That's where the Weekman family lived in the mid 1800's. They began to hear strange noises which scared them. Who kept knocking on everything? They couldn't figure it out or even catch the prankster.

One late night, as the family slept, the eight year old daughter woke up from something cold against her face. Often, when home alone, her father would hear a voice say his name. Then, a ghost appeared to the hired help. Frightened out of their wits, they all packed their belongings and moved.

Before long, a new family occupied the home. It was Mr. & Mrs. Fox with their two daughters, Catherine, twelve, and Margaretta, who was fifteen. The girls began to lose sleep at night from unexplainable weird noises and happenings that came from within their bedroom. It was so scary that they were forced to move into their parents' room.

That didn't put an end to the strange noises and spookiness until the day they heard the wind rattle the sashes. Mr. Fox checked the two sliding panels of their bedroom window and found them to be loose. Catherine watched her father shake the sash once and heard 'that knock.' When he shook it twice, two knocks followed...It was not the same sound the sashes had made nor an echo. It was the identical knock that had baffled them for so long.

Now, Catherine wanted to try and figure it out. She snapped her fingers and played her favorite game— "Do as I do." She discovered that this invisible player could interact with her. Each time she asked it to follow her directions to count, it would respond with a correct number of 'knocks.' She later made gestures without uttering one word and it reciprocated. That proved to her that it could also 'see.'

Margaretta clapped her hands and wanted to join in to help unravel the mystery. She instructed the ghost to respond to her specific requests for claps and counts. It rose to the bait with preciseness and accuracy.

Mrs. Fox decided to ask it for answers to specific questions about its personal life and her own. For example, she asked it to rap out the ages of her seven kids in order. To her surprise, it gave an extra rap because it 'knew' about a child that she had lost. It was smart!

"And that is how communication began." (3)

The Fox family told a local lawyer about everything. Naturally, it hit the newspapers which aroused curiosity. Meanwhile, Mrs. Fox continued to communicate with the entity. Through her questions and its use of raps to answer, she discovered it was not human but spirit.

She gradually invited the neighbors over to see for themselves. Each showed up a bit afraid while others thought it must be a prank. The spirit created sparks about the supernatural, but, naysayers and skeptics held their own opinions. Close neighbors vouched for the integrity and conduct of the Fox family knowing they would never deliberately try to play tricks on anyone.

Through further questioning, it was discovered that this was a thirty-one year old male spirit of a peddler with five living adult children and a deceased wife. Someone suspected that he was murdered and buried in the basement. It boiled down to nothing much being found but chicken bones.

The Fox home became crazy with spectators. Even though they lacked privacy, they didn't want to give up. Before long, the Fox sisters moved to Rochester to regain their lives among relatives.

"The rapping followed them, but that's another story." (3)

THE FOX FAMILY EXPERIENCES BECOME INSTRUMENTAL

The development of Spiritualism was important to my mother although she may have skimmed over a few details, dates, people, places, and things in its history. But, my mother wanted me to be 'well-rounded', and didn't mean I should eat more to become a chubbier child. Mom intended to increase my awareness of the growth in this area and foster an understanding in the sequence of notable events. As always, she related the significance of her storytelling with our mediumship gifts from God.

Public interest in the stories about the Fox family's communication with spirit became instrumental to Spiritualism. This phenomenon fostered credibility to additional detailed accounts of the Spirit World.

Mom stressed that storytelling and journalism were the first rough drafts of history in Spiritualism. The road was paved by writers whose unbiased chapters provided exposure to knowledge, understanding, and growth of the spiritual realm.

The establishment of the NSA and its declarations respectfully resonated with my mother. It's beliefs are shared as follows:

The National Spiritualist Association of the United States of Churches (NSAC) first formed as the National Spiritualist Association of the United States of America (NSA) in Chicago in 1893 to promote Spiritualism and educate the public. One goal was to help non-Spiritualists distinguish genuine from fraudulent mediumship, which was rapidly proliferating at that time. They also functioned as a foundation to increase communication among Spiritualists and prevent legal prosecution of spirit mediums under fortune telling and medical licensing laws.

NSA's first leaders were W. H. Bach, Harriet D. Barrett, Luther V. Moulton, James Martin Peebles, and Cora L.V. Scott. In 1899, a six-article "Declaration of Principles" was adopted by many Spiritualist groups. Three other articles were added at later dates:

1. We believe in Infinite Intelligence

2. We believe that the phenomena of nature, both physical and spiritual, are the expression of Infinite Intelligence

3. We affirm that a correct understanding of such expression and living in accordance therewith constitute true religion

4. We affirm that the existence and personal identity of that individual continue after the change called death

5. We affirm that communication with the so-called dead is a fact, scientifically proven by the phenomena of Spiritualism

6. We believe that the highest morality is contained in the Golden Rule: "Do unto others as you would have them do unto you."

7. We affirm the moral responsibility of the individual, and that we make our own happiness or unhappiness as we obey or disobey Nature's physical and spiritual laws. 1899

8. We affirm that the doorway to reformation is never closed against any soul here or hereafter. 1909

9. We affirm that the precept of Prophesy and Healing are Divine attributes proven through Mediumship. 1944

The NSAC has two educational institutes, the Morris Pratt Institute in Milwaukee and The Center for Spiritualist Studies in LilyDale, New York.

Morris Pratt Institute was built and designed by the founder as a temple and a school for Spiritualism in 1888. At the Ninth Annual Convention of the NSAC in Washington, D.C., Morris and Zulema Pratt presented a letter to the NSAC offering them the property to be utilized "for educational purposes."

The Center for Spiritualist Studies in Lily Dale is located on the grounds of the NSAC- / chartered Lily Dale Assembly, the world's largest Spiritualist camp. The goal of the center is the training of Spiritualist Clergy, Teachers, Mediums and Healers. (3)

Mom kept me up apprised on other key developments including: The Spiritualist National Union; International Spiritualist Federation; International Women's Day: Women Spiritualists; the Colored Spiritualist Association of Churches; and the Arthur Findlay College.

SPIRITUALISM'S DECLARATION OF PRINCIPLES—SIMPLIFIED FORM

My mother was always aware of updates that evolved such as in the following declaration:

- We believe in God.
- We believe that God is expressed through all Nature.
- True religion is living in obedience to Nature's Laws.
- We never die.
- Spiritualism proves that we can talk with people in the Spirit World.
- Be kind, do good, and others will do likewise.
- We bring unhappiness to ourselves by the errors we make and we will be happy if we obey the laws of life.
- Every day is a new beginning.
- Prophecy and healing are expressions of God.
- (Adopted between 1899 and 1944) (4)

My family's life didn't necessarily adhere to the above list of principles. They didn't consider themselves as "Spiritualists." History was still in the making. Around the time of the above document's origination, my mother had just graduated high school. Keep in mind, there were no computers, internet, or social media back in those days. It was a pure tried-and-true old world frontier at home and a wild-west for Spiritualism.

My ancestors and parents were good, law-abiding citizens who attended the local Catholic church on Sundays and returned home to the hard work on the farm. One family member in each generation was born with the "Gift" and used it in God's name and honor. We believed in God and always put Him above all. We saw His expression through nature in everything that God did or didn't do for the crops and in the spiritual signs sent and seen.

The principle declared above, 'We never die,' was interpreted differently by our family. I was taught that 'we eventually die,' but Spirit comes through to guide us into a spirit life.

The final declaration stated above: 'Prophecy and healing are expressions of God' would immediately have been clarified by my mother. To her, God was considered as the one and only one who did the healing through a doctor. My mother never would have considered using anyone other than a certified physician.

ADOLESCENCE

I attended Catholic school for twelve years and was raised by a strict Catholic family. I did not use my psychic medium ability much during this period in time but served as an altar boy in church. My parents were very active and involved in our religious education.

In private, Mom tutored me on what she knew about our 'Gifts from God.' Any time I witnessed Mom do readings, it was as a favor to others. She never took money. Back then, it was not acceptable to perform readings in public. But, Mom was instrumental in the continuation of the generational bloodlines and passed down the psychic know-how. Throughout my childhood, she would play games to entertain my brother and me. Little did I realize, at that time, that Mom had a purpose, and how valuable her instruction would become.

Mom deliberately taught me the essentials necessary for success—if and when I chose to practice using my gifts as a psychic medium. For as long as I can remember, Mom always used a red deck of Bicycle Standard Playing Cards in mediumship. She wrote buzz words, like: success, careful of deceit, focus on your desire, love, romance, finances...on each individual card. I automatically committed her numerous techniques to memory and sat nearby to observe how she conducted her readings and interacted with clients. When Mom passed at 82 years old, she passed on the set of 52 cards to me. I continue to use them in readings to this day.

Before Mom passed in 2010, my wife and I were at her deathbed. I'll never forget that day. Even though she suffered from brain cancer, she pointed her crooked, arthritic index finger at me in front of my wife and shook it in my face. "You overcharge and I'll haunt you!" I gave Mom my word of honor and vowed to keep my prices lower than the majority of my colleagues.

As an adult now, I am grateful to my mother for my valuable upbringing of religious beliefs and superstitions. I was taught that the "Gift" is God-given and to respect it. She emphasized that the ability be used only for good and to relay messages of importance or comfort.

"Always know that God is with you when you do readings," Mom would say. "Do not do health readings. You are not a doctor or God." Her reminders are adhered to during my readings.

I was always taught that prayer is powerful. We are to 'pray to God' for His help. But, we may 'ask our angels' for help for they have special favor with God.

ADULTHOOD

After high school graduation, I attended Clarion University of Pennsylvania and majored in the legal side of Human Resources. My studies focused primarily on sexual harassment, discrimination, disciplinary action and complaints which led me into the workplace.

I occasionally used my "Gift" to guide me while on the job. I was able to see aura's, the energy fields around people. To me, their colors reflected if clients were lying or sincere. If the aura was bright orange or red, it indicated a liar. A light blue, pink or emerald green aura gave me to know if individuals were genuine or deceptive. My interpretations never jived with textbook meanings. Specific colors were capable of holding a different connotation in comparison to another. It took me years to be comfortable with what the colors signified to me. I even learned to trust myself enough to have used these energies for my personal benefit when it came to my selection of physicians and specialists.

During this period of time, I didn't have time to use my spiritual gifts as much as preferred. A full work load consumed my days. Besides, I wanted to keep it out of my professional life. I barely had time for mediumship let alone a social life.

But, in 2006, I met my wife through a matchmaker friend who set us up on a dinner date. During the dating process, Jan and I were watching TV one night. I casually mentioned something about a large white German Shepherd. Jan's eyes grew wide when she realized I knew things about the pet she grew up with. At that moment, I confessed to her about my "Gift." She thought that I was as cool as I considered her to be.

We married in October of 2008 in a Catholic church in Akron, Ohio. During the ceremony, I looked up and spotted my father, in spirit, in the distance nodding his head in approval. Since that day, my wife has been my rock of support, acceptance, and encouragement.

THE TURNING POINT

When I was 37 years old, my father's passing kick-started my professional life into high gear for serving the Spirit World. It began with a dream I had a night or two before his death. I saw my Dad with an extremely stern face. "Get moving!" he said. That stirred my soul. I knew exactly what he meant by that. I needed to switch careers.

On Halloween of 1999, I was in Akron when I got the phone call that Dad only had hours left to live, if that. I packed a suitcase and grabbed my funeral clothes. I had a two hour drive to Oil City. While I was driving on Interstate 80 near the Grove City exit, my car filled with the most disgusting smell of rotten eggs. I looked at the clock. It was 1:35 in the afternoon. I 'knew' Dad had gone to the Spirit World. Immediately, my cell phone rang. My brother, John, confirmed that Dad had passed at that exact moment.

Over the next few years, I focused on using my abilities and serving the Spirit World. I explored skills beyond what my mother had taught me so that I could be as polished as possible. That's when I signed up for classes, and became a certified Reiki Master and a Massage Therapist. In no way did I ever claim to be a medical healer, like Mom always cautioned me against, but rather a spiritual one to be performed 'bona fide' meaning 'in good faith.' Reiki channels healing energy through the laying on of hands. It commonly begins with the head and travels down through the body's seven spiritual energy centers or chakras. By the release of energy blockages in these areas, energy is promoted which enables higher levels of spirituality, peace, and balance. This was a new concept to my mother, but she regarded it as meaningful and respectful—as well as intriguing. For once, I had the pleasure of teaching her something!

I find it interesting, but not unusual, that Spirit sends me 'flashes or images' while clients enjoy a peaceful, relaxing energy massage. It may lead to a brief conversation or something more intense. In my first experience, when I touched a middle-aged man's upper arm, I received a mental flash. I relayed that to the gentleman on the table. "Your father's gone?"

He was face-down on his tummy with his lips squashed into the massage table. But, he managed to muffle, "Ten days ago."

"What's with the redbird I see?" I asked.

He giggled and lifted his head a smidgen. "My mom now observes one almost everyday on the back porch...."

Some spirits are relentless to use any opportunity to get their messages delivered–even if in the middle of a professional massage.

Mother was a grateful soul. She always thanked Spirit for being with us to help communicate any message. Mom always said that people needed to hear what God had to say—the reason I willingly reach out to anyone at anytime an opportunity presents itself with a spirit presence. Mom was a real stickler for what she believed in, didn't stray far from her strict ways, and wouldn't expect me to either.

MOM'S MYSTICAL DEATH

Eleven years after my father passed, I lost my mother at the golden age of 82. The circumstances surrounding her last days were unforgettable. They, too, were moments that taught me more about the "Gift" that Mom and I came into the world with and the one she was leaving with.

Doctors diagnosed my mother with brain cancer in February, 2010. As her last request, we took her home to make her comfortable and allow her to spend her last days of her life where her marriage had begun in 1949–with my father in Oil City, PA. That is where she wanted to be. Now that my father had been gone since 1999, Mom would have been lost if she was unable to occupy her time with dear friends. Being born and raised there, she had a lifetime accumulation of them.

We brought a hospital bed in for Mom and put her in the extra room just off the kitchen. Hospice workers were scheduled full-time to provide their expertise. John and I would take turns taking care of Mom, one week on and one week off, as her main caregivers. We wanted to spend quality time with Mom and ensure one of us would be there when she passed.

Donna, a friend of the family for years, was hired a few weeks in as a private duty nurse twenty hours each week to care specifically for Mom's bathing and hygiene needs, for modesty and comfort purposes.

Everybody tried to keep Mom alert and engaged in activities to offer a quality of life during those days, not just an existence while waiting to go, as often happens in nursing homes and hospitals.

I always had a pot of coffee on the stove for the ladies who would visit and cheer her up, whenever they wanted to stop by. In these klatches, Mom really loved to talk about the good old days.

Rose was a people-person. She made close acquaintances and friendships throughout every aspect of her life. Foremost, Mom enjoyed her home, cooking, canning, and spending time with her family and friends. But, she was great at juggling time for her numerous pastimes in the church and community.

In addition to working for Mellon Bank North until she retired in 1987, she was a lifelong member of St. Joseph's Church and belonged to the Rosary Society. She was active in the church having served on the Bereavement Committee Pastoral Council and with the Helping Hand Group. Rose was co-founder of the Prime Timers and served as president for many years. She belonged to the CD OF A and volunteered with the St. Elizabeth Center. Also, she was a member of the Y.W.C.A. Gallivanters and the Oil City Art Council.

Rose wasn't an only child. She had one brother, Bill, and five sisters who gradually preceded her in death. Phillip and David were her two grandsons; Jillian and Allison were her great-granddaughters.

As I grew up, I had witnessed my mother's constant attention to her personal calendar marked with events and important dates. It was not surprising to me that the day after her cancer diagnosis, she began to parrot, "Is this the 28th?" or "When's the 28th?" It didn't make sense to me. I chalked it up to her regimented past routine.

Over the months, Mom tended to tire out and take longer naps in between her friends, meals, and personal care. Some days she moved about and on others she stayed in bed except for trips to the bathroom or showering. Women continued to congregate around her bed and sip hot coffee.

One day, when Mom really started to go downhill, I walked into the room to see fourteen females all reciting the rosary! I stole a private moment and sat outside on the porch. The seasons had drifted like the fall leaves that swirled all around me.

Soon it will be winter again. One year since Mom's diagnosis.

Snowflakes had similarly twirled and blanketed the windshield on our ride home from the doctor's office on that bitter wintry day.

That's when Mom developed an obsession with a need to know the day's date. I don't know why I didn't think to ask her about it. At that time, I thought it had to do with the cancer's effect on her brain and memory.

Like clockwork, Mom awakened the very next morning to the light of a new day and asked, "Is this the 28th?"

"Not yet, Mom." I replied. "Today is the 26th of September." I opened the drapes and let the warm sun stream in across the foot of her bed. I sat in a plush chair ready to help her open a pile of mail.

Nestled under the covers, she shivered. I got up and tucked her in tight underneath an afghan Grandma Elizabeth had once crocheted for her. "Do you ever feel your Mom's energy in her stitchwork?"

She closed her eyes. An enormous smile crossed her face. "Yes. She's right here, right now." Mom gently rubbed her finger tips across the woven fabric. "Oh, I see the party's getting ready to start!"

"Who's all there?" I asked.

Mom suffered with macular degeneration. Her vision hadn't been up to par for quite some time. Rose's eyes were loosely shut. Both eyelids fluttered a bit. Her cheeks blushed rose, like her name.

"I see your dad, my mom and dad, Grandma Maria, my sisters—Theresa, Antoinette, Mary, Alice, and Louise—my cousins—all of them!"

I leaned forward, my elbow planted deep into the armrest. "What are they doing?"

Mom sighed. "Sitting at the table. Waiting." Her frail hand groped the air to find mine.

I wrapped my fingers around hers. A picture of those relatives popped into my mind. "Oh, okay. That's good." They're preparing for her return home. I kissed Mom's wrist. "Are you looking forward to seeing them again?"

"Good Gracious! Yes I am." A euphoric smile swept her face. She reached across her body with the free hand. Her tiny thin fingers rubbed and stroked mine. She began to softly hum a song from her childhood. I joined in. It was one of the old ninna nanne, or Italian lullabies, of our foremothers. Through my psychic senses, I felt Grandma Elizabeth and Great-Grandma Maria's presence surround us moments before they appeared on opposite sides of the bed. They sang along in unison. It soothed my soul.

When we finished the lullaby, I acknowledged that 'as spirit' I knew they worked for my contentment by showing themselves only after I felt them, but, 'as grandmothers' they would never startle me. With a wink, they stood silently, in wait, before they vanished.

By their visit, I 'knew' it was any day now. Any time. I leaned in closer. I gently embraced Mom in bittersweet realization. With Mom's warm breath against my neck, she whispered. "Son, is this the 28th?"

"No. Today is still the 26th." My thoughts stirred. Energies reeled. Could the 28th be 'the day'? How could she know? God? I was always under the impression that nobody, but God, held that sacred knowledge. Did mediums earn an exception or special favor with Him in regards to their Spiritual Gifts?"

September 28, 2010 arrived in the wee hours of the night. I was self-absorbed in deep sleep in a room close to my mother's. Dad showed up in my dreams. He was surrounded by a glaring silver white light.

"Greg! I'm ready," he shouted. "I'm ready. I'm ready!" He vanished.

Immediately I awakened. I raced across the hall to check on Mom. She was sleeping peacefully. I kissed her warm forehead and proceeded to the kitchen to make a pot of homemade wedding soup, Mom's favorite. I found calmness rolling mini-meatballs in my palms and tending to the aromatic chicken stock.

Donna arrived. She gave my mother a sponge bath and got her dressed for the day. Mom had been bedridden for about two weeks and was no longer able to feed herself. Donna fed her a light breakfast, then read the newspaper aloud.

The pot of wedding soup was ready by lunchtime. I put a bowl of it on a tray and headed out of the kitchen to feed Mom. When she saw me, her face beamed. "Today is your Dad's birthday!"

"You're on the ball, Mom." I said. "That completely slipped my mind."

Donna tidied up the room and chatted while I spoon-fed Mom. She commented on Rose's perkiness and that all charted vital signs were within the normal range. Donna was about to leave her in my care, as was the daily routine, but planned to finish the dishes first. She assured me that she'd return for the normal bedtime schedule.

Mother's skin instantly paled. She grew weak. Donna rushed to Mom's side and checked her pulse rate. It had dropped. I phoned our parish priest. I informed him of the short time frame hospice had given and how Mom's condition suddenly worsened.

Yesterday, the hospice nurses had visited. They said to expect Mom to pass any day. But, they weren't God. Only He knew the day, hour, and the second that would happen. Anyways, she had been doing much better that morning. And, for once, she didn't ask me the date. She knew it!

Father J. rushed over to administer Last Rites and prayers. He and a parish assistant entered Mom's room where Donna and I waited with her. She was very calm and aware. I vividly remember that during the prayers, the small room became extremely bright. We all paused and stared at each other. When the priest was finished, Mom sighed. I thanked both men for their services and escorted them to the door.

When I returned, everything was calm and quiet. Donna kept vigil at the bedside with Mom's hand in hers while mother drifted in and out of sleep. It was about 1:15 when I noticed Mom's lips were severely chapped. Donna and I looked everywhere but couldn't find the ChapStick.

Mom was resting comfortably so I decided to run to a nearby corner store and buy a new tube. It would take no more than five minutes. Donna agreed that it should be okay. I whispered my plans in Mom's ear.

"Okay. Goodbye," she mumbled.

When I returned home and entered Mom's room, Donna was praying Mom's rosary beads. Her head lifted. "She just passed peacefully thirty seconds ago at 1:20."

I leaned in and kissed Mom's forehead. At least her last words uttered were 'goodbye.' I called my brother to let him know. It would take him several hours to get back to PA from NY. The next calls were to inform the hospice unit, the funeral home, and my wife.

Hospice arrived swiftly with support, comfort, and assistance in preparation for the funeral home. The funeral director came and transported Mom. We gave him a garment bag of burial clothes she had prepared a couple years ago—dress, underwear, and new slippers. Generations remained superstitious that one's feet needed footwear to get into Heaven.

But, there was no bra. I guessed Mom meant what she always said, "I wore a brassiere all my life. I will not be buried in one!"

Things became hectic with phone calls going out and sympathy calls coming in. Before long, we were at the funeral home picking out the casket—gray metal with a pale pink lining. In the blur of the moment, the calling hours and funeral arrangements fell into place. There would be the standard viewing: one on Thursday evening, two on Friday, and her burial on Saturday.

In our family, no person was to ever be buried on a Friday. Christ died on that day of the week. We respectfully believed that the rest of us were not worthy. Even though we could have held her funeral on Friday, I knew it wasn't a good idea.

Mom was very active in the local Catholic Church. Five priests celebrated her Mass of Christian Burial at 9:30 Saturday morning at St. Joseph's Church. A Concelebrating Entombment followed at the cemetery.

I didn't recall any occurrences from the psychic metaphysical side during that time. Mom must have been busy with her welcome home celebration in Heaven. For me, the transition without her in my life was a challenge. I dearly missed her.

On a brisk October day, three weeks after Mom's funeral, I was driving in the car. The windows were rolled up and I had the heater on the lowest setting to stay comfortable. My mother came to mind.

Aloud, I said, "Mom, give me a sign that you're okay." Suddenly, my car filled with the scent of Stargazer Lilies—her favorite flower. "Great validation, Mom... Thank you. I love you!"

Knowing that I could continue to communicate with my mother and other loved ones, at any time, added comfort. I felt blessed that she had given me such a rich understanding and perspective of God and His Spirit World which eased my physical loss in her transition onward.

SUPERSTITIONS

Coming from a background of old-world mediums, it's not surprising that I became strongly ingrained in superstition. In preparation for any spirit communication, I have always laid out meaningful and very personal objects on the table. In no particular order, they include my mother's pinky finger rosary with a cross along with Grandma Maria's cemetery dirt (out of respect), a vile of Holy Water, and a small Saint Benedict medal. I keep Saint Michael, the Archangel, beside me as a protector. He's the one I always call on for protection during my readings.

I also put out a silver dollar keepsake in memory of my father's death on October 31, 1999. He had collected glass jarfuls throughout his life.

The last gift that I gave to my Mom, before her passing in 2010, was on Mother's Day. That silver locket, containing a photo of my brother and me, is always placed next to Dad's coin. It holds deep gratitude for Mom "showing me the ropes" and our special bond we shared in using God's blessing of "Gifts" to help others.

A small piece of red ribbon to keep away the 'evil eye' is with me at every reading. This superstition is said to ward off evil if a strand is tied around a doorknob at a housewarming, or on a crib before a baptism.

I was taught that cloves thwart evil. To this day, I keep a bag of blessed cloves with me when I do a reading or a house cleansing. In the latter, I then give them to the homeowner. The evil eye was a common belief in Italy where my great-grandmother originated. The evil eye often gets cast upon someone by another evil glare while unaware bringing injury, misfortune, or disease. If a person thinks they were cursed with it, use a lighter and light a clove. Then, say this short prayer to get rid of it. "Jesus Christ, have mercy on me." If the clove pops or bursts, it means the evil eye was cast upon you. As the clove explodes, the evil eye is released from the one in question. Otherwise, it burns normally. The Italians call it the 'Malocchio.' For protection, people wear various good luck charms. One of mine is Saint Michael.

ANGELS AND SPIRIT GUIDES

I find a special comfort and strength in Saint Michael, the Archangel. He is the patron saint of firefighters and police officers. Mentally, I armor up like St. Michael. I visualize him taking his sword to clear away obstacles in the way and feel his protection surround me. In certain situations, I often hear my mother's voice remind me to protect myself with all angels and saints. Saints are angels.

Ever since I was old enough to kneel each night by my bed, I faithfully recited this prayer:

GUARDIAN ANGEL PRAYER

Angels of God,

My Guardian Dear

to whom God's love

commits me here.

Ever this day

be at my side

to light and guard

and rule and guide.

Amen.

According to my background in Catholic school religion classes, the word angel means 'messenger.'

Angel impression taken by the homeowner of the residence located West of Cleveland. It was validated through a reading as being sent by the sister at her deceasement. It was accompanied by a meaningful scent of orange blossoms which filled the room.

They have existed since Creation as servants and messengers of God, assigned at birth to each of us to walk closely beside us on our personal journey. They help us avoid spiritual dangers and prepare our way to Heaven—as the little voices in our head who offer guidance. Fans of Pinocchio and its song, "Always Let Your Conscience be Your Guide," liken it as being their 'Jiminy Cricket.'

As Pope Francis said, "Whenever we hear a little voice in our head saying, 'Well do this. That would be better. You mustn't do this...' Listen! Don't turn against him because it is the guardian angel's voice." 5

"No one walks alone," Pope Francis says, "and none of us can think that he is alone, because 'this companion' is always with us." 5

The Pope reminds us to pray to your guardian angel often. "Listen to the angel's counsel because he or she is always trying to defend us, especially from evil, just like a real friend—a friend we do not see, but we can hear," he says. (5)

'Angels' were divinely created and never lived on Earth.

Humans, however, can be 'spirit guides.' Those who died come to help us too. Our guides are able to switch roles depending on our needs and their expertise. One time your spirit guide may be your next door neighbor, a former lover...not necessarily a relative. We can have more than one spirit guide around us at all times.

At any time, we can always ask them for help and intercession. Remember, saints are angels. They never tire of hearing me ask, "Please help keep me safe...Thank you!"

Angels have special favor with God. "My requests to them are slightly different, "Please ask God on my behalf...Thank you!"

Ultimately, I worship only one being, God. He is the one I pray to for all my needs and thank for answered prayers.

A FRIEND TO THE END

An anonymous client shared this story to offer her insight and inspiration:

My childhood friend, Rachael, was overwhelmed in tears and despair as she returned from a doctor's appointment. The final diagnosis was small cell carcinoma breast cancer. She had moved in with me after an abusive relationship. I had welcomed the companionship over an empty nest situation. That was ten years ago.

Rachael was an active, energetic, optimistic soul who added sunshine to my life. Someone to engage in activities, that as roommates enriched one another, from taking a walk around the block to a vacation destination. We became soul sisters sharing in a bond of thoughts, emotions, beliefs...about anything and everything.

My friend remained at home throughout her battle with cancer with home health care visitors scheduled periodically. I did everything I could to keep her spirits high, to comfort, ensure the best care, dignity, and quality of life under the circumstances.

We both held a deep abiding faith in the wonders of God. Rachael viewed death not as a calamity but as a triumph. She knew her days were numbered; biblical devotion and prayer remained a part of each. Rachael occupied herself with television, music, board games, puzzles, audio books, and gourmet food parties with friends, neighbors, and family. She retained her firecracker personality until mere days before she passed.

That last morning, she awoke no longer able to render strength and opposition against the disease. Rachael could not push back the pain that seized her frail body. She surrendered. At her request, I telephoned the doctor and drove her to the hospice unit. She talked about their fabulous care and of the experiences her dying mother had once received there.

There she was, on that deathbed, with heavy doses of pain medication and compassionate nurses to constantly monitor her vital signs. She drifted into a comatose state. I felt grateful that before that happened, my hand had cradled Rachael's. We had prayed and shared some lucid conversation as she was comfortably cocooned in a wad of covers. Cancer might take Rachael, but it could never take her soul.

Rachael whispered, "I feel my mother and God close by." She sighed. "I do not fear death, but look forward to my destination." She squeezed my fingers. Her droopy eyelids fluttered. "I'll watch over you from Heaven." That was the moment she fell into a deep sleep.

The late afternoon sunlight filtered in across the small room and illuminated the dimness of a table lamp. Shadows cast upon a framed picture of Jesus which hung on the wall. The room and hallways were quiet and peaceful. A nurse assistant seated herself directly outside the doorway. She busied herself with paperwork while she kept a constant vigil on Rachael.

The Hospice unit welcomed visitors around the clock. Even so, I had no intention of leaving Rachael alone during the night. I kicked back in the guest recliner and wrapped a throw around my shoulders. I dozed off into a very realistic dream.

Two angels sang and danced about the room. "Get ready! We're all going to Rachael's welcome home party."

Rachael slipped out of her hospital gown into a pink party dress. An angel outlined her lips in cherry red. "It's time to move on to a new place." She skipped barefoot to the closet and stepped into a pair of glittering stiletto heels. "I wonder how long it takes to get to Heaven."

A spirit presence, in the exact likeness of Jesus, transpired from His picture on the wall. He took Rachael by the hand. Swish! They magically evaporated in the glowing rays of the rising dawn.

A nurse gently shook me. "Wake up! Rachael slipped away—peacefully—in her sleep."

"I know. Jesus and angels came and took her with them—to the party." I yawned and glanced over at Rachael's body—lifeless in bed. I tugged at the lever, at the side of the chair, and sprung forward. I hesitated to stand until I rubbed out a cramped kneecap.

The nurse's head instantly flinched back and an odd expression painted her face. "What? You knew it? How could you? She just passed!" Her marble eyes glared.

"Somehow, I 'knew.' She switched worlds in my dreams—it felt too real not to be true."

Two hospice workers stood by Rachael's bedside. "Want to say your goodbyes?" one asked. "Then we'll prepare her for the ride to the funeral home. You're the designated person responsible to inform the immediate family, right?"

"Yes. Consider those calls made." I got up, kissed Rachael's forehead and said a prayer over her before heading to the hospital coffee shop.

When her kinfolks were phoned, their main focus was on the inheritance items they stood to gain. The funeral service produced sprouts of greed and squabbles. Rachael didn't have much, but each pitiful last cent and possession, became their personal tug-of-war between rights and entitlement. I shook my head in disbelief.

Rachael and that crisp dream remained alive in my heart. She had blessed me with a priceless inheritance, of sorts—keepsake memories and spiritual connections. I believe she had entered into my dreams to offer up comfort and witness of her 'leaving town for good,' as she'd say. That wondrous dream. To me, it was a glimpse of her final glorious moments on earth and a wondrous moving on.

Occasionally, I'm reminded that my home was the battleground in Rachael's fight with cancer. The aftermath changed my routine. Absent was her presence, voice, laughter, conversation. Void were the empty chair at the table, an unoccupied spot on the recliner and spare bed. Brimming were our photos of special moments shared.

I continue to seek strength in my faith along with Rachael's conversations, now relayed through periodic psychic readings. This spiritual demonstration of God's phenomena is one of His greatest gifts and blessings to those left behind.

Journalists and authors have reported various stories on angels at one's death. Images of them have been captured by cameras. As a psychic medium, I have witnessed and validated accounts of angels from believers who all hold similar truths. Loved ones should not be forgotten or forever mourned but celebrated by memories and spiritual visits which keep them alive in our hearts and connected to us for the rest of our days. The greatest 'loss' is that of hard-boiled skeptics.

BEING A PSYCHIC MEDIUM

As a child, I learned that I was both a psychic and medium along with the differentiation between them. To me, there are separate connotations to the words psychic and medium. 'Psychic' is using the tools such as my oracle cards or dominoes to look forward intuitively. Psychics can only interpret the tools of their trade.

Unlike psychics, 'Mediums' have direct communication with Spirit. It is a tool often used in combination with psychic tools. As the saying goes—all mediums are psychics; but not all psychics are mediums.

Some folks are psychic mediums but use no additional tools to enable communication during a spiritual reading. They rely on and trust their God-given abilities to communicate messages in what they see, hear, feel, sense or taste including the faintest fragrances sent from loved ones.

Spirits work with a medium's contentment and peace of mind. If they know that a psychic medium becomes frightened by seeing instantaneous images of the deceased, they instead work through another one of the basic senses or in dreams.

Spirits can show up in my head or pop up directly in front of me. Personally, I would rather them be visible in my head rather than turn around to have them appear in front of me. That tends to startle me. Most spirits try to appease. But, some have less choice depending on how much energy they have to come through with. It requires much more energy for a spirit to appear before our eyes than in our heads.

Keep in mind that on the Other Side, we hold the same personality and communication skills we possessed on Earth. Those loved ones who could connect emotionally with others while here physically tend to be better communicators from the other realm. Those who kept to themselves seem to have a lower level of energy and more difficulty expressing themselves; as they always did. Some don't even care to keep in touch. Again, the personality doesn't change much.

PSYCHIC MEDIUM READINGS

My mother's generation could not openly and publicly conduct readings. She held them privately to help others and honor God and her 'Gift.' Many residents in our community knew and asked, "Why have a reading?" Rose responded, "People need to hear what God has to say."

A reading is simply a casual sit-down of a psychic medium and a person for the purpose of a spiritual communication with deceased loved ones, spirit guides, or a check in on beloved pets. Spirits welcome any opportunity to communicate. They enhance our happiness and quality of life by providing peace of mind, clarity, guidance, inspiration, and responses to a myriad questions.

Mediums can read a person's past, present, or future self because they are in tune with the Spirit World. I read and relay the energies and messages of the Spirits that come through. They usually give the person sitting for the reading a message of comfort that they are happy or content on the Other Side.

Sometimes they pass information about the future to loved ones. Often, a Spirit will tell the sitter what to do, but not always. They generally offer subtle choices to guide one's paths yet respect free will in decision-making.

TIPS FOR READINGS:

1. Have an open-mind and open-heart.

   Arrive free from negative effects of drugs or alcohol so you can get the most from your sitting and not waste your money in a foggy state of mind. Spirit usually sets the stage by gaining the trust and confidence of loved ones. They validate through the medium how they died, or report facts and events from the sitter's daily life as evidence that they are with them and watching.

2. Don't be afraid of what they may say.

   I often find some clients apprehensive that loved ones remain precisely who they were, even into the afterlife. Personalities don't change much, but, people can and do change in death. Because of self-reflection of a past life necessary for eternal soul growth, individual views shift and soften. Spirits become more compassionate, caring, and loving. They're no longer judgmental, abrasive, or abusive. They offer help and benefits; not hindrances.

   Instead, they are now the best version of themselves— free from all earthly stressors, distractions and negativity. They communicate out of an abundance of love to guide and give us comfort, peace, and joy necessary for their own soul progression in the afterlife.

3. Take along pen, paper, iPhone, or recording device.

   Arrive that day with any questions you want to ask already jotted down. Most mediums encourage clients to record the reading. It can offer clarity and greater understanding at a later time. Please devote the highest respect to Spirit World communication. Wait to resume personal cell phone conversations or texting until after the session has ended.

4. Pray or communicate aloud before the meeting.

Hours ahead of the appointment, say a prayer or talk to your beloved to set an intention. The Spirit World will start to plan for the spirit and the message to be brought to the table to help you on your path for your highest good. Most clients let me do my work. It allows me to connect to the first spirit who comes through bearing a purposeful intent.

If your heart is set on speaking to someone in particular who does not come through, they may have a weaker energy level or be waiting in the background behind those most eager. Be certain to make mention of that special one. Mediums can ask the Spirit World of their whereabouts and they may be called ahead for a chance to speak.

5. Always conclude with gratitude and thanks.

I was taught to view readings as a rare, holy, spiritually enlightening event. Spirits speak in symbols, emotions, analogies...in ways which suit a medium's contentment for interpretation into a clear message. God's work is the reason I was born a psychic medium. It goes way beyond money or ego; I am a servant of God and the Spirit World. I was properly instructed at an early age to always thank Spirit, which applies at any age.

FINDING A MEDIUM

How does one choose a medium? Discerning which psychics and mediums are authentic, or not, can be a trial and error experience. One can cold call any number found on the internet, an ad, or a random business card. The risk for a satisfactory outcome is often a gamble. Some individuals get scammed while others get lucky. Try the following suggestions:

• Take a look at the medium's website. Check the reviews along with the number of followers and 'likes.'

• Ask people you know for the contact information of professionals they use, like, and trust. Word of mouth is usually the best advertisement.

• Initiate conversations with your questions and listen to what others share about their spiritual experiences.

• Watch and listen at public demonstrations to observe psychics and mediums in action—through gallery readings, spiritualistic churches, psychic fairs and expos, videos, audio recordings, or ask permission to sit in with a friend while they have their own reading.

• Allow your intuition to be your guide.

PSYCHIC SYMBOLS

There are a variety of symbols I receive psychically during a reading. The following symbols are unique to myself and the spirits. I interpret them similar to a hand gesture, or seeing an emoji during the communication. Any word or symbol can have several different meanings depending on the context and can add clarity to the message. Mine tend to be consistent and helpful but I don't rely entirely on symbols. They could expand at anytime because the Spirit World is never stagnate.

- A bright sparkle—Indicates that another psychic medium is present.
- Car wheel, or driving—Signifies to be careful when you are driving; past or present car trouble or accident.
- Bible—If I'm shown a Bible, the client may need to reconnect with their faith.
- Itchy palms—Means someone should be using their hands for a craft or in a creative way–art, design, construction....
- Nausea—If I feel nauseous, it tells me the cause of death may have been cancer somewhere. A shortness of breath signifies lung issues, chest pains are indications of heart problems.
- Rosary beads—Someone is helping you from the Other Side; praying for you; or asking for your prayers.
- Roses—Always a good sign of someone feminine from the other side, usually a motherly figure. White roses may be offered by the spirit around celebrations, anniversaries, and birthdays, or sent as an apology.

• Scales of justice—This can mean everything is in balance; but when scales are tipped means something needs to be fixed to regain balance.

• Thimble—Someone is or was a tailor or liked to sew.

• Triangles—If perfect means things are in order; when tilted to the left or right means somethings are off balance and does not have a good foundation.

• Tight throat—Someone has something to say, it's "stuck in their craw." Often, a tightening around my throat accompanied by a sensation that I can't catch my breath indicates someone was hung to death.

• White lace—a strong indication of a female figure who has passed that was very feminine. It may indicate a wedding or a birth.

• X—means NO. If I see an X through a liquor bottle, it means someone has a drinking issue.

HE WANTS HIS TEETH

A lady from Ohio came to me for a reading. I sensed the presence of a male spirit around her. His passing seemed recent. She barely got seated when he began with a stern message.

As straight-faced as I could muster, I passed that on to the daughter. "He wants his teeth!"

Her eyebrows squished together. She gave me a blank stare. "I have no idea where they are." She bit her lip.

"Oh, your father isn't as upset as it appears," I said. "He's actually laughing about it now."

She shook her head and looked upward. "Thank God."

"Your dad says that the teeth buried with him do not belong to him."

"He shows a symbol for 'home.' Would they be there?"

The lady shrugged her shoulders. "Well, he died in a nursing home." She paused. "He really doesn't need them anyways, does he?"

"No," I said. "It's just his way to let you know it's really him communicating with you."

"Oh shit!" she said. "That explains why that nurse called me the day after Dad's burial—looking for his roommate's dentures. She asked if I had them among his belongings."

She shook with hysterical laughter. "They won't believe it when I tell them where they really are."

SUSPICIONS

I was having a reading with a middle-aged woman which began with oracle cards. I kept getting cards that indicated lying and deceit. Marilyn, the sitter, looked oddly at me with raised brows. All cards centered around the 'bride card' which means marriage.

I asked, "Are you having any marital problems?"

Her face soured.

"Bella," I blurted.

Her eyes widened and her face reddened.

"This girl I see seems awfully young," I said. "Is she a 'problem child', of sorts, in your marriage?"

Marilyn clutched her heart. "Holy shit! My suspicions WERE right about my husband and Bella having an affair. My God! She's 24 years younger than him."

My jaw dropped.

She abruptly stood and grabbed her purse. "Thank you, Mr. Nicholas. I can't wait to confront those cheating liars!" Marilyn stomped out of the room.

THE ATHEIST

Vibrant autumn leaves drifted like parachutes in the smoggy Cleveland air. From the window, I watched my next client make his way across the parking lot. He clutched his hat and garments in a sudden gust of wind. I was rather amused. A door slammed. Momentarily, he stepped inside and scraped a hand through a gray, disheveled mane.

I stood.

"I have an appointment with Greg," he said. He rubbed his chin. Instinctively, his hand graced mine in a firm handshake.

"Pleased to meet you. Have a seat. We'll get started."

He cleared his throat and inhaled a couple short breaths. "I'm Karl."

"Have you had readings before?"

Karl's head dropped. He rubbed his thick thighs. "No, it's my first. I don't really believe in religion or mediums. I just wondered if I somehow could talk to my brother, that's all." His head slowly lifted, his eyes skirted around mine. He stared out the large picture window.

A younger male spirit eagerly engaged me. I mentioned that to Karl. "You almost backed out and didn't come. Right?"

Abruptly, Karl's head snapped back to me. Our eyes leveled. His body stilled, facial features frozen, mouth agape.

"Y-e-a-h," Karl slowly mumbled.

"Your brother is here, resembles you a lot. He shows me money. Do you OWE him?"

Karl gasped. His head dropped. "Yeah. Several hundred." Tears welled in his inner eyes. With short jerks, he tugged at the corner of a red, cloth handkerchief stuck in his skintight pants pocket. It didn't budge much. He dabbed his eyes with a shirtsleeve, instead.

"He wants me to tell you, 'It is forgotten.'" I said. "He's glad you're sitting here."

Karl nodded.

"What's with the big golden dog? Oh! He says, 'Buddy's with me!'"

Karl let out a huge sigh of relief. "Good to know. Those two always did have a bond." His voice softly drifted. "I b-e-l-i-e-v-e—"

"What's that?"

"In what you do. A higher power MUST exist." Karl stood straight with his shoulders back. He rubbed his goose-pimpled forearms. "That HAS to be my brother!"

I nodded. "And you have many 'others' waiting to speak also."

"Wow! We really don't die." Karl grinned. "Words can't thank you enough, Sir. See you again." He tossed a fifty on the table, waved an arm in the air, and was out the door.

I leaned back in my chair and thanked his spirit-brother for his message and presence.

The validation from the brother, in spirit, led Karl in a new direction. His belief in what mediums do drives my commitment to help people, like him.

Karl came to grips with a heart-felt affirmation and a mind-consciousness that life does continue after death. The realization that those physically 'gone' are spiritually 'present' after death—capable of participation in one's daily life —became clear and evident. We are all spiritual beings having a physical experience. Karl's 'evidential reading,' inspired him to schedule again.

Spirit communication has a potential to heal any fractures of the heart and soul and offer love, strength, and healing. Even if people have never been to a psychic medium or may never have this opportunity, they, too, receive spiritual signs.

My mother always believed that any after-death communication with Spirit is a sacred experience. We can somehow feel when their energy is near. She always reminded others to look for the many ways that Spirit speaks to us, by any means imaginable, to gain our attention through, but not limited to:

- Angels
- Bible
- Coincidences
- Daily life events and experiences
- Dreams, visions, flashes
- Epiphanies
- Family
- Friends
- History
- Holy Spirit
- In our darkest hour, in silent moments
- In our hearts, thoughts, senses
- In nature's beauty and inspiration
- Meditation
- Memories
- Miracles
- Opening and closing doors
- Orbs
- Phenomenon
- Photography
- Prayer

- Psychic Mediumship
- Signs-animals, birds, butterflies, clouds, coins, feathers, felt touches, flowers, orbs, wind chimes, numbers, smells, sounds, electrical fields (lights that flicker) or electronics that act weird from the interference from spiritual energy...
- Songs
- Synchronicities
- Through other people
- Voices
- Whispers
- Writing

God uses various ways to spread His beacon of light for an awareness, transparency, and preponderance of spiritual evidence. It's a humble nod to God's Eternal Creation.

THE TOOLS OF THE TRADE AS A PSYCHIC

Psychics, or intuitives, receive messages from Universal Energy, which includes a client's personal energy, or aura. Their ability is best used for psychic guidance. They are able to confirm to us what our own intuitions are telling us so that we can trust our inner wisdom. The tools I use as a psychic include oracle cards, seashells, dominoes, tea leaves, and palmistry. Each is an instrument of fortune telling or divination, the practice of seeking knowledge of the future or of the unknown by supernatural means.

After I use any of these tools, I mentally cleanse them with golden white light to get rid of any evil or negativity.

ORACLE VS TAROT CARDS

To me, oracle cards are more open to interpretation. There are many different types such as Angel Oracle cards, Native American cards, and Crystal Oracle cards.

I do not use tarot cards because I am uncomfortable with them. They don't click with me for the desired connection. These cards have set meanings and regardless of the design of a Tarot deck, the meanings are the same. To me, oracle cards are a better version and resonate well for my purpose.

Oracle cards originated from oracles—people considered wise, insightful, or prophetic who use inspiration from God to predict the future or help with current situations or problems. The oracle's purpose is to empower one with wisdom to make changes that one seeks in life.

Every now and again, a card flies in the air landing near the table's edge or sometimes on the ground. That 'jumping card' always gets my careful attention and scrutiny.

My Mother's Deck of Cards

My mother passed down her personal deck of regular playing cards to me. What makes them 'special' are the significant cue words hand written by her on the border of each card. I find that these cards or my oracle deck always work in unison to back up and lend support to my interpretations of dominoes and seashells.

Seashells

Seashells have been used as a psychic tool for hundreds of years by the people of the Mediterranean area. Shells are connected to the water and water is emotion. Each shell in a spread of six can tell a story about a client's emotions and feelings.

I keep 46 shells in a wooden jewelry box that once belonged to my mother, Rose. The seashells came from more than one beach—a collection from the sands of Egypt, Morocco, Greece, Italy, the Mediterranean, and all around the world. Shells were used over generations for both divination and fortune-telling.

When I use them, the client begins by selecting six shells. Then, their unique story unfolds through my intuitive interpretation of each choice.

- a spiral shell means running around in circles
- a bumpy, ugly shell means to take better care of oneself

• a sand dollar means a message from someone
• a broken shell means cracked emotions; disappointments

DOMINOES

To begin a psychic reading using dominoes, I instruct a client to pull six dominoes from a satin bag. Each domino has a meaning and when put together in a spread of at least six, tells a story. Our family's set contains dominoes that are blank through 66.

The sitter places each tile, dots down, on the table. Each domino holds meaning and adds to the clarity of the reading. I instruct the individual to turn each one over, dots up, giving each piece their energy in that transaction. Then, I arrange them in order from lowest to highest. Sometimes, if I feel more clarity is needed by Spirit, I will have the client pull an additional domino, as necessary.

I always use dominoes as a tool in conjunction with oracle cards to achieve the best synchronicity and integrity in the communication. This was another one of my childhood games; Mom's clever way of passing down the family's know-how. I enjoyed our playtime and automatically committed her techniques to memory. When I began using my ability as an adult, I found these skills to be second nature and effective.

Dominoes are said to have originated in India around 1120 AD then made their way to China before reaching Europe and America. (6) When the 18th century saw the "game of domino" surface in Europe, it first appeared in Italy. (6) That is where my great-grandmother, Maria, experienced this old world tradition, on the mountain top of the Monte Cassino Abbey, before she immigrated from Naples to the United States. Domino tiles were first used for fortune-telling and divination long before they ever became a popular game. It was one of the oldest tools used by oracles in their communications from God.

Tiles are also known as bones, tickets, stones, or spinners. The reserve of dominoes is often called the boneyard. The highest tile is double six and the lowest is a double blank.

Regardless of the origin or size of domino sets, they all are capable of producing a domino effect in effective intuitive communication when used as a psychic tool.

TEA LEAVES

Reading tea leaves is a form of scrying where images appear that carry a meaning. For example, a ladder means move up. A tree means growth. A butterfly signifies moving on in some way.

PALMISTRY

I read palms. Not only do I read the lines on the palm, but, by touching the hand, I feel the person's energy. To me, the lines on the palm change from one year to the next with life experiences. Palmistry not only includes the lines of the hand but also the changes of the fingers and knuckles.

THE TOOLS OF THE TRADE AS A MEDIUM

If I am strictly operating as a medium, I use my mediumistic abilities to communicate directly with Spirit in the presence of the sitter who desires more of a visit with a deceased loved one. This is known as a reading or mediumship.

The divination tools I use which require the direct communication of a medium include psychometry, séances, and gallery readings:

PSYCHOMETRY

One of my strengths is the use of divination in psychometry. With this unusual insight, I am able to discover facts concerning an object or its owner through direct contact or proximity to the object. Please allow me to clarify the meaning of 'trickster' and 'divination' used in Laura's story, which illustrates psychometry.

A TRICKSTER is a spirit who moves or hides objects, bangs, knocks...anything to seek attention.

The word DIVINATION comes from the Latin word 'divinare' meaning 'to foresee' or 'to be inspired by a god.' To practice divination is to uncover hidden knowledge by supernatural means. It is often associated with mediumship, the occult, and fortune-telling. (7)

The first time Laura came for a reading, her hands were not empty when she entered the room. She quickly sat across from me. Onto the table, she placed a tiny one half by two inch clear, glass, corked bottle, wrapped with a short piece of twine strung through a hole in a seashell. It appeared to be a sand souvenir from a beach vacation.

Beside it, she placed a worn, five inch long, toy replica of a blue station wagon. It was scorched on a side panel. The client slightly tipped it revealing two partially melted tires.

Laura said, "This was rescued by its owner from a kitchen fire." She moved the bottle atop of the car's hood.

I asked her to give no further information and please separate the two objects. She complied. I would first ascertain their single meanings or identities and later connect them in spiritual communication if I found a relationship between the two items. We began.

"A male spirit is present," I said. "He tells me that you two have been friends. It feels like a long time. Nothing romantic, just friendship. He recently passed. About a year, I'd say. He's happy you brought something of his along with you."

I pointed to the blue car. "Is that his?"

"Yes," Laura said, "It's Marco's."

"Can I touch it now?" Upon her nod, I pickled it up. "I'm getting he was a lonely fellow. Especially on holidays, but says, 'I was included.' Tells me you are very sincere, and that you two looked out for one another. He's appreciative of you."

With a fixed gaze, Laura's neck tipped back. I continued.

"Now that he's crossed over, he's with you, watching you. He's kind of a trickster, a prankster. He hides things. Does that make sense to you?"

"Oh yeah," Laura replied. "It sure does. That's Marco for you! I couldn't find my charger for my watch. So, bought myself a new one. Then, I found the old one in the corner of the laundry room under my mop."

We chuckled. Marco laughed too.

"He's now snickering about shoes," I relayed. "Does something with them. Understand that?"

She giggled. "He and I tricked out all my old high-heels. I wanted to wear the peacock ones today, but have a problem. Can't wear them."

"He's in agreement," I said. "Can you hear him laugh when it's still and quiet? He's 'with you', he says, 'with you.'"

She thoughtfully nodded.

"Who likes water, the lakes, boats?" I pointed to the vial on the table. "Can I touch it?"

Laura gave permission. I held it up and peered through the glass.

"One male writes the word 'water,'" I said. "I'm getting that the man fond of it is in here. 'But not alone,' I'm told. 'Together, at peace.'" I repeated spirit's words then deeply inhaled and exhaled. "Did the other two in here know the other one?"

Laura straightened. "They're all related. It's my brother's cremains, the one who loved Lake Arthur and Geneva on the Lake, plus my aunt and uncle, who are brother and sister."

I tucked in my thumb and raised my hand. "I see this number but not getting why."

She chuckled. "The four of them ride everywhere with me. I keep them in my car on the dash."

That makes sense now." I sighed. "Their energy is so bloody strong. Did you invite them to come?"

She cocked her head sideways and cupped their belongings with her palms. "Maybe, when I brought them inside with me."

"I'm hearing a female. She wants you to know—'No more falling or dizziness.' Does this make sense to you?"

Laura cracked a smile. "My aunt."

"She's been waiting to say hello and sends you her love," I said.

Our session was up. I walked her to the lobby. On the way, I explained that her reading exemplified an exercise in psychometry.

Laura mumbled phonetic sounds trying to repeat the new word. She held her palm out and glanced at the objects. "I'm impressed by what you figured out with these! I'll be back again."

APPORTS

An apport remains a phenomenon where spirits materialize or move objects. Many believe a spirit, such as a deceased loved one, is the giver of the item which carries a symbolic meaning for the receiver. I like apports. Spirit can place them in our way that we are sure to notice. They are gifts.

A few years ago, I received one in the parking lot of a massage practice. I was going to see Barb, a religious long-term client. From time to time, she commonly would hand me small items such as rosary beads or a pocket Bible. One day, when I stepped out of the car, I bent to pick up a small wooden cross lying at my feet on the pavement. Just then, my phone rang. It was Barb's daughter. She told me that her mother had just passed. I 'knew' the cross was from Barb!

One of my female clients had an intriguing experience. She shared the details after a spiritual reading. She had planned a get-away with her husband to Las Vegas to relax and gamble. The 2020 global pandemic struck. The trip was canceled. The world quickly halted normal routines to heed the CDC's (Center for Disease Control and Prevention) stay-at-home and quarantine mandate to slow the spread of the deadly virus.

This housewife became bored with the confinement to her house. She decided to discard the junk in the living room end table. To her amazement, one of the first things she pulled out was a small black velvet pouch with draw strings. When she opened it, she discovered over-sized silver dice. She showed them to her husband and questioned him.

"Where on earth did these dice come from and who put them inside this drawer?"

She impulsively rattled the dice in her palms, blew on them for good luck, and rolled them across the kitchen table yielding two fives. She shouted to her husband. "A pair of sunflowers!" The casino atmosphere came alive in her imagination: the warble of slot machines rotating electronically, players sitting on edge, punching buttons, coaxing a win, while sipping cocktails and smoking cigarettes...

Her enthusiasm and pretense drew her partner into a crap game which lasted well into the night. They referred to a cheat sheet of nicknames for calling thirty-six dice combinations: 'Snake eyes; Six one you're done; Puppy paws; Easy eight...'

The couple sharpened their skill and jargon of slang terms for crap numbers using unique stories as mnemonics for memory. For example, a 'Jesse James' related to a 4-5 combination because he allegedly got shot with a .45 caliber pistol. The 'Ballerina' was two 2's associated with 'tutus.' A 'lumber number,' a 2-4 combo, identified with 2-by-4 boards.

It was later validated through a reading that one of her beloved spirits intentionally left the dice as a gift, or apport. She couldn't understand how that was possible, but thanked Spirit for creating such a memorable time. One may wonder how a non-physical spirit was able to produce a tangible object but that remains a divine mystery in our interaction with the Spirit World.

Séances

Spiritualistic séances, in the presence of a medium, have been associated with appearances of apports. Some of the séances aired on television touted white doves to be apports but were proven to be ploys to increase ratings and deemed fraudulent. I personally have never had a spirit bring or send an apport to a séance.

Generally, people think of séances as a conjuring up of evil spirits. I stay clear of that. My séances are always conducted with respect and never to contact evil and darkness. I keep this event very friendly, simple, and comfortable for guests. I always try to calm any fears or concerns that may arise. They are different than those you may read about or witness in various videos. If anyone desires anything negative or evil to come through, they are in the wrong place! Participants are escorted outside if in possession of unsafe Ouija boards, or like paraphernalia.

My séances are respectful spirit communications intended for the benefit of connecting loved ones. They are conducted with divine protection as a 'message event.' I'll walk you through the typical format. It all begins, before it begins, before I enter a room filled with eager clients. That's when I seek out a quiet place to sit and ask spirits what I need to know for those in attendance. They may send me verbal messages, symbols, or anything they desire to aid in the communication. Knowing that I'm not starting off blindly, I'm prepared to meet an awaiting group of seven to twenty people. More than that maximum number of guests can be very tiring and overwhelming for me.

Darkness or a dimly lit séance area is my preference. As I introduce myself, I light white tapered candles. I prefer to use that kind since it is easier to see the flames bend, flicker, spark, or jump. The color and number of them is not important to me or the purpose.

I instruct everyone to put one hand on the table and keep it there for a continuous energy connection. There is never any hand holding. My upbringing called for keeping things very simple, relaxed, and comfortable for the guests. Many people express discomfort in locking hands, and germs, with total strangers.

We open with the recitation of The Lord's Prayer: "Our Father who art in heaven, hallowed be thy name. Thy kingdom come. Thy will be done on earth as it is in heaven. Give us this day our daily bread, and forgive our trespasses, as we forgive those who trespass against us, and lead us not into temptation, but deliver us from evil. Amen."

We then recite The Unity Prayer of Protection: "The light of God surrounds us; The love of God enfolds us; The power of God protects us; The presence of God watches over us; Wherever we are, God is! Amen."

The room quiets. I can hear a pin drop aside from someone fidget or an occasional tap of a foot against the floor. Those in attendance sit straight and alert around an oval or round table. Eyes open, close, blink. There's a muffled sigh, belch, or sneeze. A fart lingers. Giggles stifle. Silence resumes and is broken by a silly low mock growl....

I'm aware that some reactions attendees may experience could result from either internal or external stimulus. Often, they see, hear, feel, or smell various signs. They may experience sensations such as a tap on the shoulder, a sudden breeze, unexplained noises, or a fleeting scent. Some shiver, stroke goosebumps...or rub the raised hair on the nape of the neck. All eyes are immediately on deck when a pen, car key, or other object moves or rolls by its own accord. The possibilities: normal gravity, spirits, or more rarely—an apport.

Cameras click. I always encourage attempts to capture entities during any of my events. In the past, various things have appeared such as faces, orbs, apparitions, or other strange anomalies that are invisible to the naked eye but wind up in pictures and videos.

I speak, "Bring in Archangel Michael to keep us safe."

Extending my arms outward I call out, "Open the doors and raise the veil between our two worlds. Ask only those to come through for our highest and best good."

Seances are 100% medium to Spirit World communication. My senses are heightened and I start with something I see, hear, smell, or feel physically or through my spiritual senses. Many times I get "flashes" of images from Spirit and that is all I get. Things come fast—as in this abbreviated recollection of one.

My eyes fix on a face across the table. "A male spirit shows me a motherly female sitting at a grave in the cemetery eating food."

Immediately a woman starts to cry. She covers her heart with both hands and offers an explanation. "My son passed away. My husband and I take turns eating there on our lunch breaks."

Another image flashes before me. "I see a young man in a leather coat. He passed in a car accident. He says, 'They left me.' He shows me a grave site with Halloween décor. I see the hands of a skeleton coming up from the dirt."

A woman laughs and cries at the same time. "It's my son Matt. We decorated his grave for his favorite holiday. Only he would know and say all that."

Messages from the Spirit World continue for at least an hour or longer depending on how many guests are in attendance.

To close the séance, I always say, "I lower the veil and close the door between the two worlds. I thank those who have come through."

I feel it is very important to remember to thank the spirits. And, I have never forgotten to thank my audiences for their participation.

THE WHITE LIGHT OF PROTECTION

Divine white light is a spiritual protection which uses the unlimited energy found in the Universe for our highest and greater good. When I feel I need it, I always pray aloud for it to surround me.

MY PROTECTION PRAYER

The light of God surrounds us;

The love of God enfolds us;

The power of God protects us;

The presence of God watches over us;

Wherever we are, God is!

Then, I take a very deep breath and visualize being surrounded by God's Divine Golden White Light and any negative energy going deep into the ground. I imagine God as a megawatt bulb emitting the clearest, brightest LED light giving protection, to myself and the individuals I'm working with—from evil, harm and negativity. This is needed for me to deliver spiritual messages for everyone's highest and best good.

Divine White Light is capable of protecting anyone at any time or place. The protection lasts throughout the entire session or event, no matter how lengthy it is, as long as I am tuned in with it. This White Light has been used effectively for many centuries as a form of spiritual protection by holy men of great longevity.

GOD'S LIGHT

With God's light, everything stems from Genesis. It proclaims that in the beginning of the world, everything was dark until God created and commanded light to shine in the darkness. He then separated light from dark and called them day and night. The sun, moon, and stars were created as limitless light sources.

White light, the purest form, is a natural combination of all the rainbow colors focused into a single spot. It is generated from the solar system by the stars and Sun but can be made artificially through LED's and fluorescent lighting. (8)

GALLERY READINGS

Gallery readings are mediumistic direct communications with spirits involving an audience presence in any large room in which people pay various admission fees to be spectators and participants for the event with no guarantee of getting a reading that day. There could be any number of guests depending on seating capacity and the draw of the speaker. Famous celebrity mediums such as Sylvia Browne, Allison DuBois, John Edward, Tyler Henry, and the Long

Island Medium have popularized gallery readings with packed television audiences.

Spirits seek me out long before the event's scheduled start time. I welcome the eagerness of these early birds and an opportunity to engage them in mediumship. I start to receive various signs that I call 'rounding up.' Prior to the event, I sit with pen and paper. I jot meaningful key words from spirits in the order they are received and personally welcome and thank each for their presence. I tend to get a mix of spirit personalities. Some linger around me with a lower energy level or have difficulty sustaining it while others zip in and out with higher vibrations.

The time ticks closer and I start to pace. My hands get a bit clammy. I wipe them with a handkerchief, close my eyes, and slowly inhale and exhale. Public speaking does not come naturally to me. It's not one of my "Gifts." I admit I'm nervous as I walk forward and scan the number of spirits and individuals within the gallery that I will be facing during the duration of the session. I'm about to rely on my "abilities" to assist both realms with meaningful communication. I pray for calm, focus, and strong clear connections to be able to accurately voice all messages for the greatest good and honor of God. I sense my mother's invisible presence and hear her words. "Remember, God is always with you during every reading. People need to hear what God has to say." Now, I am good to go.

Unfortunately, not everyone will have the opportunity to hear from a loved one. People are people, dead or alive. Those spirits with the most dominant personalities tend to be in the forefront of the afterlife with a 'pick me first' attitude. "The squeaky wheel always get the grease," as the saying goes, and "It is on Earth as it is in Heaven." From here to there, personalities don't change much.

It seems that those humans with a tendency to always be 'first in line' usually sit in the front rows. I smile and look across the gallery at people seated and the others who are pushing their way in to find a lucky spot. I can't help but giggle to myself when I focus on the spirits around me—likewise competing for my attention and chance to speak with loved ones, much like their earthly counterparts.

The audience's collective body language and silence signal to me that they're settled and ready. I rarely need a timepiece to tell me when it's time to begin. I welcome and thank them for their attendance then make a brief introduction. I glance at the top of my list where I had jotted my first key word, 'my first time.'

MY FIRST TIME

Soon after I had arrived for a gallery event, held at a local banquet center, the first guests arrived. A younger male spirit followed closely behind his parents as they entered the room. I greeted the couple then engaged their son in my customary spirit-welcome and round-up. His energy level was low. I ignored a strong impulse to offer a private mini-reading with the trio before the gallery session started, but hesitated. I trusted that he could maintain enough energy to power him through, if, I began with him. I stuck to my routine and jotted an impression, 'my first time,' at the top of a blank page in my notebook, and assured the young spirit of his placement.

And now, it was now his turn. I stepped toward a seated couple in front of me. Their eyes riveted as they attentively leaned forward and the male spirit towered over them from an empty spot in the next row. His energy level waned but he exposed the contents of a clutched hand.

"Your son is gone," I said. Their eyes watered.

"He says, 'My first time.'" The mother began to cry hard and his father turned his head. I explained that I was being shown a fistful of pills. His mother nodded.

The young spirit appeared shy, remorseful, and said little. I wasn't certain if he meant it was the first time he actually experimented with drugs, or his first deliberate attempt to overdose, so I followed my intuitive senses. "To your knowledge, was this your son's first experience with drugs?"

Though a veil of tears they mumbled that 'they thought so.' I passed on that it was their son's 'first time' to participate in mediumship. He struggled to maintain energy and had begun to fade.

"Your son wants you both to know that he had never done anything like this before. He says it was accidental. He's sorry for the pain it caused. He blows kisses."

The husband cradled his sobbing wife in his arms.

I gave them a minute to compose and focused on the Spirit World. "Another male—who passed not long after your son—stood by his side throughout his message."

The father's face brightened. "Could it be our friend Jake?"

"This man wants you to know that he's now cancer-free."

"That's him!"

The wife's eyes opened wide. "I'm sure glad to know they're together."

I questioned the husband. "So, you drew something—a picture?"

He unbuttoned his shirt and laid his hand over a heart, smothered in artwork. "Yep. My son will always be right here. I'll never get him out of my mind or off my chest. By the way, this was 'my first time'— for getting a tattoo."

Stop Yelling At Me

The next spirit intention on my list was 'yells.' Immediately, a gentleman in his late 70's, I'd say, appeared in my head, as he had done earlier in my round up. His message was for his daughter who was seated in the audience. He showed me a symbol—a tortoise and a quick-hopping hare.

Visible to me, he swayed back and forth behind this lady, in her fifties, who sat in the second row. He was ready to say what he came to say.

My eyes leveled with the attentive woman. "I see an older gentleman around you dressed in bib overalls. His was a 'fast death.' Does that make sense to you?"

She quickly clapped her hands to her cheeks. "Has to be my Dad. He died in his sleep."

"Are you taking care of your mother?"

She nodded.

"Your father rolls his eyes," I said. "Is she a real handful?"

The woman released a heavy sigh and spoke sternly. "Yeah. Some days Mom's more than I can bear. She's difficult and tries my patience, but I do the best I can."

"Your father says, 'Stop yelling at me! I'm dead!' Do you yell at him?"

"Yeah, all the time, for leaving me stuck here with her."

I giggled. "Trust me. He hears you loud and clear."

INKED

The next word on my list was 'ink.' I re-established a connection with a particular female spirit and waved my arm toward the location in the audience where Spirit stood waiting for her opportunity to communicate through me. The spirit-being, a motherly figure, shared resemblances in facial features to the girl seated next to her.

I needed to introduce evidence that supported a connection to the two by validation of the spirit's personality, a shared memory, how she passed, or anything spirit choose in order to authenticate her presence to the loved one. Spirit mentally gave me an image of an engraving tool and an etching.

"Who recently got a fresh tattoo?"

That same young gal raised her hand.

"Is your mother in the Spirit World?" I asked.

"Yes."

In my head, the color yellow flashed and an imaginary insect flew past me. I made a quick interpretation based on my intuitive skills. "Is your tattoo a yellow butterfly?"

The girl nodded and pushed up her sleeve.

A deep sense of pride filled me as the spirit saluted her daughter. "Your mom says she was with you while you got it done. You are a real soldier. She's so proud of you!"

"I'm home on leave from the military," she said. "I got the skin art yesterday in her memory. Thank you, Sir."

"No, thank you for your service, Ma'am. God Bless!" I said. "Trust that your mother is always at your side. Pay attention to her touch. She wants you to know that she kisses your cheeks often and always sends love."

THE VETERAN

Even though I had previously 'rounded up' some spirit connections, I take spirits as they come through to me. A veteran who had already made his presence known to me stood respectfully beside me from the start and waited his turn. I received a strong signal that he was ready.

"I have a veteran who's been standing here waiting to say hello," I said. "I feel he's coming through to a granddaughter." I passed that on for the audience. "He shows me a cemetery and a young lady leaving him something small, yet very huge, at his grave. He's not giving me what it is."

In the gallery, a young lady in a red hoodie straightened in her chair. She learned forward and covered her mouth with her palm. Her hand dropped. She scanned the audience but didn't see a raised hand or hear a response. She grinned and waved her arm high into the air. "I think that's for me! I went there yesterday. I can't believe how you actually know this?"

I winked. "He shows me a piece of paper and says he appreciates your words."

She blushed. "I wrote him a poem."

"He sends his thanks and love. And, wants you to know he is not at the grave but with you anywhere and everywhere—'just a thought away,' he says."

Time passed quickly with continued mini-readings. Before long, an usher neared with a silent clap. It was my cue to wrap-up the event. I thanked the audience and the Spirit World for their attendance and participation.

HOUSE PARTIES

A house party is a great place to invite a few friends over for psychic entertainment to eat, socialize, and experience private readings. The 'reader' may either be a psychic or a psychic medium. These individuals will use various tools of their unique trade and preference to facilitate communication.

ON YOU

I turned off the highway into a driveway lined with pine trees just like Mable described when she booked her private house party over the phone. I expected to do readings for a group of about twelve guests.

Siri announced the location, "Arrived." I pulled up behind several parked vehicles and pushed my gear shift forward. The curtains parted. Cheerful guests peeked out and waved from a two story Cape Cod. I barely opened my car door when a teenage boy raced from the patio.

In a flash he stood before me, arm extended for a handshake. "Hey Dude. I'm Cody. Welcome!"

I shook firmly. "I'm Greg Nicholas."

"Hear them?" Cody said. "Squawking like a hen house in there." He put a finger to his temple and spiraled it outward. "They're all nuts over you and this party." He escorted me.

I chuckled. "So, I'm the star of the show?"

"Better than being a party-pooper like me," he said as I stepped toward the threshold. "Enter at your own risk, Dude."

The ladies welcomed me the moment I set foot in the kitchen. Mable, the hostess, introduced herself as did each guest, in turn. Graciously, they extended their hospitality and invited me to help myself to the spread of appetizers and beverages on the buffet table. I appreciatively indulged in some chips and dips.

After the hoopla of my arrival, things settled down. So did I— at a quiet table in the corner of the living room with Sally, as the first guest-reading. This stylish lady, was probably in her mid-sixties, judging from her salt and pepper hair. She sat quietly clutching her hands, rocking in place.

I began dealing oracle cards, throwing them down on the table. I stopped in mid-action, put the cards down, and my eyes met hers. "There is a gentleman here with a close connection to you. Feels like he's been passed about a year, give or take. He made it. He wants you to know 'he made it.'"

Sally threw her palms up, slapped them together and interlocked her fingers. "Oh good, he really made it! He made it!" A trickle of happy tears dribbled down her cheeks.

"Were you worried that he didn't?" I asked.

She clutched her stomach and slightly bent forward. "Yes, afraid he hadn't crossed over."

I began to stammer and repeated his words, "I'M ON YOU. ON YOU. WEARING ME."

Without hesitation, I stared directly at her. "UNDERGUTCHIES?" I leaned in closer and whispered. "Do you understand what he means by that?"

Sally blushed. She untucked the shirt from her sweatpants and stretched the elastic waistband. Low and behold, she had worn her husband's white Hanes underwear to the party.

I never underestimate what I might hear or see in my line of work.

THE TWINS

On the drive to any house party or event, I adhere to a disciplined personal regiment. The radio is never turned on. I prefer silence to tune in with the spirits who often accompany me.

"What do I need to know?" I ask them. "Please give me clarity."

That Saturday, on my way to Mable's party, I picked up on two young male spirits. They both appeared at the same time. I received a sign that they passed in their twenties. I sensed they knew each other well. My head started hurting. That signaled to me that their deaths involved head injuries and possible trauma. I got nothing more until the party got under way.

When I arrived, I asked Mable if she knew about the 'young deaths.' She startled and began to nod. I told her not to tell me anything about it. The first two readings went well but neither of the two males appeared at all.

Then, came a third reading and one of the two men showed his presence again. A lady and her eighteen-year-old daughter sat in front of me. I winced and rubbed my head. "I feel severe pain in my head. I'm getting that it's connected to a young male who's around you." Both women became teary-eyed. My eyes fixed on the eldest. "This is your son?"

"Yes."

"He passed instantly from head injuries," I said. "He didn't feel any pain."

The two embraced and cried. "Thank God," the mother mumbled.

"I'm getting that this happened quite recently."

"Four months ago," the daughter added.

I informed them that he and another young man rode with me in my car on the way there. They cried harder. The mother shouted for another guest, Anna, to join us. An older lady hurried to their side. That's when the other young male spirit re-appeared and stood next to the first one. I informed the females of his presence.

The ladies quickly updated Anna.

"I'm getting that both of them passed quickly, together." Now, all three cried. "They want you to know they're at peace." I paused to make sense of a symbol, but wasn't sure how to interpret it. "Would you understand the meaning of a motor bike?"

Anna spoke. "The two of them, Matt and Mike, are brothers. Identical twins. I'm their grandmother and this is their mother and sister. The boys were riding dirt bikes and crashed into each other head on."

"I'm genuinely sorry for your loss," I said. They thanked me.

As an empath, I felt the hurt, pain, grief, and suffering so raw within these women.

"They mention the writing on your skin," I said. "Does this make sense to you?"

One by one, they each managed to roll up a sleeve. "We all got memory tattoos."

"They laugh about the horses," I said. "Did one twin once purposely spook the other's horse causing it to buck him off?"

The three ladies exchanged glances and giggled. The grandmother nodded. "It's always brought up when we talk about days gone by," she said.

"Yeah, I turned gray when I saw the horse dragging one upside down." The Mom ran her fingers through her hair. "In that moment, I thought I lost a twin forever. I prayed hard to God."

The sister pulled up an iPhone picture of her brothers. She pointed out Matt and Mike—mirror images of each other. "You probably can't tell me which one spooked the horse?"

I had no clue until the twins helped out. "It was Mike—on the right."

Anna chimed in. "WOW. How'd you know that?"

I winked. "Matt showed me scars on his elbow and hip—from a coal black horse."

The sister held her arms out wide as if to hug the world. Her eyes sparkled. "I have to admit that I was skeptical. It's our first experience doing this. I didn't know what to expect. But, knowing now that the twins are still with us is priceless—this reading is the best time and money we've ever spent. Thank you!"

My own mother popped into my head. I sensed her unconditional love and appreciated her words. "I'm happy to see you always do your readings for the highest and best good. You make me proud."

BABY MATTHEW

At another house party, I had arrived early before guests streamed through the door. I casually chit-chatted to John, the host. Suddenly, a young spirit came through and told me his name.

"Matthew is here," I said.

John froze. His eyes instantly welled with tears.

"You lost a little boy?"

He nodded.

"He's clutching a blanket." I added. "But, he's presenting himself to me as a few years beyond a newborn."

John nodded. "Even though my boy was six, I buried him with his favorite 'blankie.'"

Such a short message with everlasting impact and healing. That gentleman became a repeat client. He always tells me how thankful he is for that initial message from his son. They continue to visit together through frequent readings.

STOP QUESTIONING MY DEATH

Sometimes, a family's unanswered nagging questions, thoughts, and bickering carry on long after a loved one is gone. Such was the case with the Casey's. The matriarch, Lily, had passed six months prior to her daughter, Bella's, first contact with me to schedule a group reading.

When I arrived at Bella's Ohio home, an elderly woman, a spirit-being, appeared to me, in the driveway. She wagged a finger. "We need to settle this matter."

Bella opened the door and welcomed me inside. I felt the spirit presence follow.

We passed through the kitchen. Tantalizing aromas sifted from the hot oven and crock pots. In the dining room, guests were gathered around a long table dotted with beverages and plates of food.

Spirit Lily, the one in the driveway, stood beside me as guests introduced themselves. The majority were her family members. Bella offered me to sit at Lily's empty seat at the head of the table. I laid out my customary items to prepare for the first reading.

I informed everyone that Lily had been with me since my arrival. "What does she need to settle today?"

Bella's sister, Alli, spoke up. "We'd all like to find out whether her death was intentional or accidental."

"Who gave her money for rehab?" I asked.

Alli spurted, "I did. She got hooked on prescriptions after her back surgery." She sighed. "I tried to help her safely get off them, without having another seizure."

The brothers voice was stern. "But, she ended up back on them." He scowled at Alli. "Said she'd never consent to going back to that place ever again! She hated it there. That's the reason why she overdosed!"

Alli retaliated. "Don't blame me! Did YOU try to help?"

I had to interrupt the argument to relay Lily's firm message. "Lily says to all of you, 'Stop your bickering right now! Stop questioning my death! It was accidental.'"

The room became quiet. Family members exchanged stares and low whispers.

"Did Lily have a sister that passed in January?"

They nodded. "Aunt Ethel."

"She's been standing beside Lily throughout this reading. 'Please start getting along with each other now', she says."

With that said, the tension was respectfully cut. Hugs, apologies and laughter followed.

VANQUISHED SKEPTICISM

Thelma had scheduled five people for a small party on Monday at her country home.

That day, the reading began with the appearance of a male spirit, around forty years old. He held a tiny baby in his arms. I immediately clutched my chest in a fleeting empathetic sensation of pain; indicative of a massive heart attack which validated to me how the man had died. I made that known to the guests.

Tears streamed down Thelma's cheeks.

"And your newborn daughter passed right after he did? From SIDS?"

She nodded and bit her lip.

"He says to please stop worrying. The two of them are okay." She cupped her hands around her cheeks.

"Did he like tools?" I asked.

Everyone nodded.

"He's showing me them and says he always had one in his hand."

A lady, that had introduced herself as Thelma's mother, commented. "He earned a living as a mechanic."

"He wants to give his best friend a message. Is he here in the room?"

An exceptionally tall, wiry guy shifted in his seat. "Me?" He leaned back in his chair and stiffened.

"He says, 'Don't lose my frigging tools!'"

The friend chuckled. "That's not the first time I've been told that by him, but never thought I'd ever hear it again."

Spirit showed me hand-sketched pieces of artwork. "What's the deal with the tattoo?" I asked.

"Honestly, I plan to get one in your memory, Dude." This best friend acted spooked and as if his buddy was standing right there. His head slowly swiveled and his wide eyes darted everywhere. "How's it possible?" he stammered.

Thelma looked at him. "Still a skeptic, huh?"

He shrugged his shoulders. "Maybe not."

Thelma said that on the day before, while she videotaped her twelve-year-old son riding the dirt bike in the back yard, she cried because her husband wasn't there with her to watch his first jump.

"'Of course I was,'" he says. "'Didn't you see me and the baby?'"

She scratched her jaw. "No. What do you mean Mr. Nicholas?"

"He wants you to pay attention to that video."

Her face blanched. "I just got warm tingles up and down my arms," she said. "Excuse me please. I gotta watch it! Where's my glasses and phone?"

I took a break to get coffee and cookies. Thelma bolted into the kitchen behind me. "I can't believe it! Look at this!" She shared a short clip of two turquoise-blue orbs bouncing alongside her son and the bike.

Psychic Fairs

A psychic fair is a paranormal event held in practically any setting and open to the general public. Various like-minded vendors offer their services, such as, but not limited to:

- angel card readers
- aura readers and/or aura portraits
- aromatherapy
- chakra pendulum readings
- energy healers
- numerologist
- oracle card readers
- palmists
- paranormal groups and guided tours
- psychic intuitive readings
- psychometry
- psychic mediums
- runes
- salt lamps
- spiritual books and author signings
- tarot card readers

Individuals with a gamut of psychic abilities sit at private tables and give visitors a unique spiritual experience. Sessions are generally shorter and at lower prices.

The main attraction is usually the gallery event, conducted by one or more popular mediums. Participants sit for a limited time in hopes of receiving short personal spirit messages from loved ones on the Other Side in these demonstrations of mediumship. Entry may be free or reasonable.

On site, there are often various vendors selling food, beverages, crystals, candles, gemstones, incense, jewelry, clothing, books, and more. Psychic fairs, or expos, can be held under one big roof or outdoors for a few set hours or an entire weekend.

It is a great opportunity for curious novices and an opportunity for skeptics to give it a try. It's a good place for enthusiasts to take advantage of special promotions and discounts. Business cards and brochures are generally available at every booth. These events contribute to the wellness of the body, mind, and soul. The venues and grounds are commonly packed with like-minded people.

Public Psychic Investigations: Communications with Haunted Hill View Manor Entities

The hour drive from Ohio to the Haunted Hill View Manor in Pennsylvania flew by in conversation with my wife, Jan's, company. The dashboard clock blinked 9:45 as we turned left off Route 65 in Shenango Township onto the grounds.

The summer's heat lingered as did the spirits. Shadows of the past greeted me as I drove up the driveway and parked. I was anxious and excited to be there for communication with the spirits. They knew and recognized that I possessed psychic medium abilities. I was their messenger.

"Welcome," cheered a spirit's voice inside my head. I sensed his presence and turned my glance toward the building. A gentleman, in spirit, appeared in a doorway dressed in a dark green work shirt and pants. He stretched his arms. One hand waved over his head and the other gestured for me to proceed toward him.

Jan and I exited the car. We grabbed a briefcase and purse from the back seat.

My wife closed the door of our sedan and hit the key fob. BEEP!

"Today's gonna be exhilarating," I said. With a handkerchief in hand, I dabbed sweat from my face. "I already feel them seeping through my veins!"

My head gradually became abuzz with a flood of spirits who tagged alongside each incoming guest that came to partake in the day's events. I temporarily blocked them. Many of these spirits would try again to catch my attention in my 'round ups' prior to my scheduled private and gallery readings. They would be eager for an opportunity to communicate with their loved ones on earth.

At one point in the itinerary, my attention would switch focus to the manor's entities during a paranormal psychic investigation of the haunted landmark to expose communications with those who once lived there and continue to do so in the afterlife. The touring public would anticipate excitement in what these entities would do or say. I assumed the crowd would be sizable. After all, this site had gained notoriety as one of the most haunted places in New Castle, with constant paranormal and ghostly activity.

I did not see my first spirit-greeter in green as we hurried across the lot. We headed toward the majestic double door entrance, framed in a cement arch, with a concrete slab above the doors engraved Hill View Manor, big and bold. The huge glass-pane doors required a strong push and opened into the main lobby. To my left, the office, it's frontage walled by sections of glass. A middle-aged woman rushed about in a black staff shirt and greeted us with our agenda for the event. She led me to a comfortable room, near the office, where I would do psychic readings. My wife got waylaid chatting with someone she knew.

It didn't take long for me to get settled into my assigned space. I went to find Jan. She sat in the lobby, engaged in conversation. It was her first time here, my second. A man with silver hair and bifocals approached me with a firm handshake and introduced himself as Hunter. He would later participate as a Hill View paranormal investigator to guide our tour group on a public haunt jaunt.

He twisted his watch. "Do you have a minute to check out the boiler room for spirits?" He clasped his hands together. "Until today, it's been temporarily off-limits due to some leak that needed fixed. Coming?"

I didn't hesitate. We strolled through a hallway with double doors and descended a musty stairway into the basement. When we arrived at our destination, Hunter stopped to unlock the door.

My nostrils seemed to flare. A woody, oak scent permeated through my head amid the mildew and dampness. I perceived the smell without the use of my physical nose but from a psychic sense–clairscent or 'clear smelling.'

"Was he a whiskey drinker?" I asked. My spiritual eyes received a symbol of an 'X' across a liquor bottle, a sign that indicated someone had a drinking problem.

Hunter nodded and pushed the dingy metal door wide open.

"How'd he get his hands on liquor?"

"Some of the workers would sneak it to Eli."

I stepped across the threshold. My eyes spotted a male spirit leaning in a far corner of the boiler room. I moved closer. *You're the same green-jeans man that welcomed my arrival from across the parking lot. Are you Eli?* His head sharply lifted and dropped.

A tightness gnawed at my chest. That indicated that Eli once had breathing or heart issues. Eli flashed a vital sign symbol of an oral thermometer—32 degree F.—which gave me clarity and helped validate his manner of death. "I'm getting that something happened with his ticker." My eyes leveled with Hunter's. "He froze to death?"

Hunter explained that Eli allegedly sneaked out of the facility one winter night for some binge drinking. Early the next morning, he was found passed out near the entrance covered in snow and ice. They carried him to the boiler room to thaw out. But his heart apparently stopped, possibly linked to alcohol poisoning.

My watch chirped. It was time to return for my scheduled appointments. On the way back, the entities tugged at me with their emotions. They were excited I was there. I felt energy waves of unmasked anger, sadness, lonesomeness, and fear.

I made it back on time. Those private twenty minute readings ended at 8:15. My wife joined me when I exited through the lobby where she awaited.

THE GALLERY READING

A staff volunteer accompanied us to the chapel for my scheduled half hour public gallery reading from 8:30 to 9:00 P.M.

The Spirits that I had rounded up earlier throughout the day reappeared. It was time to clear them from my head space, one-by-one, so I proceeded with their messages. "I'm getting a strong whiff of flowers," I said. "A sweet, rose-like, citrus scent. I'm seeing the color pink."

The lady to my right waved her hand. "Mmmm...I smell them too! My sister recently passed. I transplanted her pink peonies into my yard...."

Then, I felt a message for the young couple, to my left, sitting by themselves. "I have a female motherly spirit here holding an unborn infant," I said. When I looked directly at them, they wiped their moist eyes. "This woman wants me to tell you that everything's okay. Now was not the right time for him."

The woman spoke up. "I just miscarried a month ago. I was not quite three months along. Thank you for that much needed message."

I didn't get a chance to catch my breath when all of a sudden I tasted tobacco. I passed that along to the audience and mentioned how unusual it was for me to receive a taste sensation from Spirit. With that said, it disappeared!

Could this be a trickster? Instantly, my spiritual tongue received a strong, rich taste of snuff with a hint of peppermint. At the same time, an image of a female spirit appeared in my head. That identical spirit stood beside a lady in orange sitting in the third row, aisle seat.

"I keep hearing the letter 'B'," I said. "Does anyone understand the association between tobacco and letter 'B'?"

The woman wearing an orange dress waved both arms high in the air. "I bet it's my grandma, Betty, who raised me."

"Did your grandmother chew?"

"Yes, every single day!" She giggled. "She sure liked her dips of wintergreen Copenhagen."

After a few more mini-readings, the usher signaled that time was up. At that point, I thanked the guests and spirit-beings for their participation and attendance. A staff member instructed everyone who was going on the haunt jaunt to use the restroom, stretch, or remain seated.

The Tour, Spirits, and Findings

I announced to the gallery participants that I would be the designated medium on the psychic investigation tour to give any messages or impressions presented by the entities. Like many novice participants that day, I was about to take a virgin tour of the building.

At nine o'clock sharp, a team of three seasoned paranormal investigators, including Hunter, took to the floor and reviewed important rules. Stay with the group. No flames permitted. Therefore, no lighting cigarettes or fireworks...if you fail to follow these do's and don'ts you will be immediately ejected from the grounds....

I stood against the wall near the audience and listened.

Hunter made an announcement. "We will be going into the basement to the boiler room where George, a former army veteran, ran the system. He was and still is an avid Steeler's fan. Don't mention any other team or he'll throw something at you. Once, he threw a football and hit a man in the head for merely wearing another team's shirt. Beware!"

Another tour guide joined the conversation. "When we get to the second floor that we call 'Angelo's hall,' we will enter his room where he reportedly passed. Please don't ask how. It makes him angry. He doesn't want to talk about it."

Instantly, I began to gasp for air and clutched my neck. My airways tightened. I couldn't swallow or breathe. I sensed my eyes bulge. A sensation of a noose bound around my throat indicated what happened to Angelo. My wife asked if I was okay but my vocal cords rendered useless. With a half nod, I stumbled to the exit for fresh air.

The grasp on my throat quickly released with no physical harm to me. It was a sympathetic pain many mediums endure in the line of duty. When I regained my composure, I returned inside to the crowd. I soon found an opportunity to interject, "Angelo hung himself. I could feel a leather strap, perhaps a belt, around my neck."

Not wanting to gain any preconceived information about former residents or of the spirits present, I exited the room again. Less data is always best in order for me to deliver a genuine read. Five minutes later, thrill-seekers swarmed from the chapel swirling bright flashlights in every direction, pumped up for an adventurous ghost hunt in the dark, dank halls.

A tour of the entire building was led by the three members of the paranormal investigative team. I followed directly behind Hunter. I had to filter out extemporaneous spirits that came along with guests from those who once spent a lifetime of confinement within those walls.

"Keep up with us," the tallest guide shouted. "You will have an hour of private exploration at the end of this tour." Naturally, the tour group tended to disperse into separate groups and converge at the end of a corridor or in a room where guides stopped to tell a story or feed common knowledge to all.

The building was truly 'alive' with the spirits of former residents. I felt like a live wire for the spirits' continuous flow of energy throughout my body. I could clearly see and hear them. My psychic clairsenses would feed me clarity, as necessary. The exception was a taste sensation. That one was a rarity to me, stimulated by a spirit when needed for enhancement of a message. I sensed an urgency to openly share any details or secrets that the spirits were willing to divulge. Would they bring 'life' to this tour?

The group stomped up and down long hospital-like hallways. Flashlights shined in and out of single rooms that residents once occupied. The second floor was known as the 'Noisy Floor' because of the spirit voices that typically coughed, laughed, wept, and screamed. Their energies caused things to bang, drop, roll, and slam.

The strong vibes of the second floor began when I walked into Angelo's bathroom. I saw an old leathery belt hung from the ceiling. Those strong sympathetic choking sensations returned again—like I experienced in the gallery. My body ached as if I had been badly beaten. My gut and psychic senses told me that Angelo had suffered physical abuse moments before his death. His loud voice echoed in my head. "I didn't do it!" I relayed that along with each detail and sensory experience as it happened.

The group was on the move again. Somehow, I zipped ahead of some stalled foot traffic. When I approached a particular room on the opposite side of the hall from Angelo's, my skin crawled with big chillbumps. Something seemed odd, out of place, uncomfortable. It weirded me out! I felt a 'leading' energy pulling me in at the same time it was pushing me out. It compelled me to enter a short, narrow entryway. There was one room, at the very end, from what I could see. Alone, I entered that darkened space and lightly groped the walls with one hand to guide me. With my flashlight, I discovered the first doorway and tried to turn the doorknob to access that room. That's strange, I thought, it must be stuck or nailed shut.

A mental image flashed of a past existence of a sarcastic soul, a bully, behind a locked door who routinely interrogated, picked on, and ridiculed others. My body became a conduit for an intense flow of energy I encountered. It raised my hair on the nape of my neck. A negative energy spiraled out in front of me blocking my path of travel. It pushed against me. My psychic instincts gave me insight that I wasn't welcome to take another footstep. Having clairempathy, I 'sensed' a strong, powerful force of emotional energy—fear, pain, tragedy—in that location. As a clairsentinent, I simultaneously 'felt and experienced' a bombshell of these three raw emotions explode within my consciousness.

"Stay out! Stay out!" came a firm shout from an entity. A silhouetted hand raised before my face, fingers fanned. "STAY OUT!"

I instantly reversed direction and headed back toward the main hallway while blinded by the oncoming flood of the tourists' bright flashlights directly on my face. I pushed my hands out in front of me to stop anyone's advancement and repeated the warning. "Stay out! Stay out, they said. They don't want us back there."

Our paranormal leaders stilled with caution. People quieted. Wide eyes became vigilant, jaws dropped. My wife bit her nails.

Psychic intrigue caused me to stutter. "I'm going back to find out WHY. Wait here."

"Be careful!" my wife insisted.

"We got your back!"

"Scream for help if you need us!"

"Will Greg be safe going it alone? Should someone follow?"

I slowly stepped forward in a cold sweat. Each breath burst in and out of me. I wiped my clammy palms on my shirt tail and clutched my Saint Michael bracelet for added strength and protection. Telepathically, I honed into the spirit realm for clarity. I called out to my mother and saints.

A spirit with a snitch personality spoke up. I sensed his compassion. "Back in my days, everybody knew what 'Stay out!' meant. If you didn't, you would be raped back there. Didn't matter if you were man, woman, child, or dimwit."

The distinct scent of Mom's Emeraud perfume surrounded me. I breathed deeply through my nose. Tension melted. I felt her armored presence guarding me alongside St. Michael. I realized that I had failed to shield myself from an energetic overload. My hyper-alert senses got me sucked into the pent-up energies, emotions, and past life woes of the former residents. But, together, we had just unleashed what they wanted to show and tell.

My spiritual 'snitch' continued to comment on past sexual abuses. He used my inner awareness to flash mini-movie like clips about what he had once witnessed. Allegedly, Angelo had been abusively raped, beaten, carried across the hall to his room, and strung up by a belt bound around his neck at the hands of the rapist to squelch threats to tattle to management. It now made sense why

Angelo never wanted to speak about it. His suicide may have been questionable in the past; but now, the truth had been exposed.

Ironically, this floor just happened to be the same one commonly referred to by certain staff as 'Angelo's wing.' Hunter moved the tour along. We passed by two spirit-beings—older fellows in an argument hitting each other with their canes. I chuckled aloud and kept pace with my own cane clicking against the floor.

At the end of the corridor, I got a vision of a wheel-chaired residents being pushed down the stairway to their deaths or suffering serious trauma at the hands of a shadowy figure with a fascination for causing harm and havoc. My psychicness gave suspect that it may have been a disgruntled person—nurse, caretaker, or resident.

That intuitive suspicion hit me hard, again, when we passed by the nurses station. I instantly became nauseous. My nasal cavity filled with an intense sweet solvent-like scent. I rarely receive 'taste' sensations from Spirit, but today I did. I had a fleeting strong chemical taste which burned like drinking a shot of rot-gut moonshine. I received this psychic information without having any actual physical source of that taste in my mouth. It was simply another psychic sense called clairgustance or clear tasting.

By the time we returned to the main floor, I received flashbacks of my parents farm in Oil City. That's when I recognized that peculiar scent—from the garage. We always sprayed the farm tractor carburetors with ether engine starting fluid to cold-start them no matter what the season.

But, why was I sent that whiff of ether near the nurses station? That thought tugged at me even after the tour had ended.

I researched the internet the following day for answers and explanations. To my surprise, I discovered that diethyl ether caused nausea and vomiting in 85% of patients. (9) I was grateful that my psychic sympathetic nausea didn't cause me to actually hurl in public! Some other side effects from inhaling ether included poisoning of the blood, dizziness, drowsiness, convulsions, pneumonia, insanity, nerve damage, paralysis, miscarriage, and damage to a fetus. (9)

I reflected on the part of the investigative tour when we stepped into a small room known as the infirmary. The entities coughed excessively. My body beaded with sweat. I cleared my throat and resisted a strong urge to cough. Being an empath, I related and felt their need to do so. I remembered it was now 2020, in the midst of a global pandemic. Even though we all wore masks and tried to maintain social distancing, I didn't want to alarm anyone with my coughing jag; a symptom of COVID-19. I hurried out of that room and waited in the hallway for the group to exit. As I stood idle, a female spirit relayed to me that there had been several unwanted pregnancies among the Manor's patients. When I had inquired about them, she silenced.

I scrolled down the web page and studied the list of ether's pertinent side effects again—'miscarriage and damage to fetus'— and began to wonder if this drug had any connections. Could it have been once used by the Manor as a magical "rag and gag" cure and cover-up? My thoughts ran rampid about this drug. Was it possible? I learned that by the time the American Civil War broke out in 1861, diethyl ether was used as the primary surgical anesthesia. The Hill View's original poor home launched six years later when ether's usage was widespread by dentists and surgeons. (9) The only way

I'd ever know the truth would be to respectfully and directly ask Spirit the next time the opportunity presented itself again.

My thoughts reeled. Before I had headed home from the Hill View that evening, I had asked employees about that excessive coughing I had heard. Scanty records did indicate that a Tuberculosis ward had once existed on the second floor. The public poor who couldn't afford a hospital, were admitted to Hill View Manor to recover. Often, children were temporarily housed on the upper floor until their parents were discharged. This was a recent discovery made by another medium through her exposure to the many spirits of youngsters she encountered upstairs.

I had questioned the owner and staff about illegal bonfire cremations because of an unimaginable part of the tour. An angry entity had appeared before me with a disturbing graphic image. The spirit showed men throwing his once human remains into an outdoor fire pit, perhaps a small bonfire. This entity was pissed off because he had actually been 'burned alive' while in a coma. The nurse did not detect a pulse or heartbeat. This injustice was probably a common occurrence during those earlier years when residents were mainly confined to the grounds. They were at the mercy of in-house medical care, and possibly, one sinister nurse or caregiver.

Nothing existed on record. The spirit's revelation was, yet wasn't, any surprise. Apparently, there were many additional misgivings that had previously gone under the radar. Accurate record-keeping was one of them. Now, these injustices were now being brought to light with the inclusion of mediums on the public psychic investigations.

Under the former operation of the Snyder family, accurate documentation of patient records, deaths, and burials were negligent and inaccurate. These managers were eventually fired for their incompetence when a severe storm swept over the cemetery and washed up many bodies from shallow unmarked graves.

The facility welcomes any facts or paranormal stories about those who once lived there. They also encourage known information from former employees, friends, relatives, and acquaintances.

Psychics and mediums serve as another tool in understanding the paranormal world which exists. With their spiritual abilities to communicate during Haunted Hill View Manor investigations, a richer history can be realized to piece together a puzzle of the past.

A Brief History of the Manor

I often frequent this landmark to participate in events such as private readings, psychic fairs, public psychic tour guide, gallery readings, and to teach an occasional class such as 'Sensing Energy and Spirits.' I enjoy the positive spiritual energy, friendly owner and staff, along with the wealth of history, paranormal activity, and incredible spirits.

What began as a poor farm in 1826 and became an extended care facility from 1977 to 2001 created a rich paranormal history from its hundreds of residents spanning decades. The manor ceased its operations in 2004 for financial reasons.

The closure forced the real estate to sit idle until a woman from Pittsburgh purchased it in 2005. Her intentions were to renovate the building into apartments or a condominium. Unfortunately, the new owner unexpectedly passed away within the year.

Upon her death, the property was inherited by the family who had no idea what to do with it. They soon heard stories from former workers of the facility who witnessed paranormal activity during daily operations. The property owners were approached by ghost hunters to explore the building.

In 2013, they began doing business as the Haunted Hill View Manor with ghost tours. This preserved the landmark's integrity and legacy as a haunted estate.

Ghost Hunter, Travel Channel's Ghost Adventures, Ghost Lab, Destination Fear, The Spirit Realm Network, and SyFy's Ghost Hunters are among the popular investigators that have visited. Using scientific gadgets, professionals and enthusiasts attempt to understand the paranormal.

Instruments used to hunt and interact with ghosts include thermal scanners, motion and infrared sensors, dowsing rods, infrared lights, EVP's [electronic voice phenomena], EMF meters to detect electromagnetic fields, night vision cameras, video cams, and LED flashlights.

While nothing has been scientifically proven about ghosts, spirits, and other strange paranormal happenings, it remains an ongoing challenge saturated in investigation, speculation, personal opinions, and beliefs. It boils down to science verses religion—a stickiness of confusion and conflict. Science is based on clear observation of physical reality which is lab testable. Many religious truths stand alone despite what science says about God's existence, the soul, prayer, Spiritual Gifts...and various other phenomena.

Paranormal encounters and activity do exist at the Haunted Hill View Manor. It's been commonly said 'that if the walls could only talk.' The spirits of former occupants have begun to do just that—especially since psychic mediums were added to investigative tours. The entities will eventually surrender each and every detail and story about life there—both past and present.

The Haunted Hill View Manor, located at 2801 Ellwood Road, New Castle, PA, has gained status on a list of most popular haunted places.

HALLOWEEN:THINNING OF THE VEIL

In my family, I was taught that Spirit can be contacted anytime. It is common though in the metaphysical community that 'the veil' is the thinnest during Halloween. The theory is that it's easier for spirits to make contact when the veil is thinner. I don't necessarily adhere to that belief, but that seems to be the common thinking in the community.

"Around Halloween, it's been said that the ethereal barrier or veil thins between our world and the Spirit World. Of course, no human or scientist has ever seen, touched, or measured this invisible, intangible existence of phenomenon. It's only a metaphor for the very thin spiritual boundary between the realms which is always easily passable for crossing over when we die or when we want to communicate with deceased loved ones. In mediumship, it is a field of energy, a filter of consciousness, where we temporarily forget what exists on the other sides of it—the truth of who we are, or were, and our eternal connections to each other." (10)

"The veil allegedly is thinner than normal from mid-September until the start of November when there becomes an increase of psychic abilities, experiences, and paranormal activity. This idea stemmed from an occult Pagan concept, where the dead crossed over to walk among us during that period of time. People began to dress as ghosts, demons, and monsters to blend in with any evil spirit that came through the veil on All Hallows Eve, the origination of Halloween." (10)

Personally, I have never delved into the dark world. In communication with the Spirit World, I call on Archangel Michael for protection and to ensure I am speaking with the intended spirit. As a child, I dressed in a home-made costume and went door-to-door on trick-or-treat night. I have always loved Halloween, Fall's colored leaves, cooler temperatures, candy apples, chocolate, and spirits!

As a psychic medium, I have not experienced any outstanding differences in communication with the spirits during this thinning of the veil, which remains entirely possible and within reason of the paranormal.

A PENCHANT FOR PHENOMENA

A penchant for phenomena has always been in my blood—an integral part of my upbringing accepted as a normal part of life. Even so, some experiences left me awestruck or speechless. As a precocious child, I annoyed my parents with my inquisitive habit of beginning every sentence with 'why' or 'how come.' Mom would say that unexplainable mysteries came from God. "Ask Him for those answers," she chirped. I realized, with age, that the world and universe had an abundance of wonders to be seen and experienced each day, even though they often went unnoticed by most people.

'Phenomena'[plural] can be defined as either natural or psychic events, occurrences, or happenings in the world around us. They can also include physical sensations felt by a person and often understood and referred to as 'appearances' or 'experiences.'

For a singular event, it is called a 'phenomenon.' Tricky words, right? Likewise, it is anything rare, unusual, interesting, and difficult to understand or explain. It too can be seen, felt, tasted, experienced, and studied with no true justification for its existence. It remains a marvel that boggles our minds.

We live in a wonderful world of phenomena to explore, captivate our thoughts, and photograph. I'd love to embark on new adventures to experience, firsthand, the numerous kinds of paranormal experiences offered through natural and psychic phenomena that add depth and inspiration to our lives as spiritual beings.

Natural Phenomenon

Natural phenomena is broader than most people realize. There are various classifications and hundreds of examples within subcategories that often overlap. As I read through this list, I pondered how many I have actually seen, experienced, or even know a thing about. (11)

Astronomical Phenomenon
- supernova
- solar eclipse
- lunar eclipse
- perseid meteor showers
- northern & southern lights
- tidal range

Biological Phenomenon
- birth
- anabolism
- catabolism
- death
- decomposition
- growth
- fermentation
- population decrease
- metabolism

Chemical Phenomenon
- fire
- oxidation
- rusting

GEOLOGICAL

- Earth's magnetic field
- geysers
- hotsprings
- rocks
- volcanoes

METEOROLOGICAL PHENOMENON

1. ATMOSPHERIC OPTICAL

- aurora
- crepuscular rays
- green flash
- haze
- ice blink
- light pillar
- rainbow
- monochrome rainbow
- moon bow
- moon dog
- rainbow
- sub sun
- sun dog
- twilight, dawn, & dusk
- water sky

•2. OCEANOGRAPHIC

- tsunamis
- ocean currents
- breaking wave

PHYSICAL PHENOMENON

- boiling

- freezing
- gravity
- magnetism

I have always wanted to experience nature's incredible phenomena. My bucket list includes a handful of destinations to explore. The magical color swirls of Aurora Borealis in Alaska intrigue me. My wife wants to see the migration of 100 million Monarch butterflies at the Biosphere Reserve 62 miles outside Mexico City. At least once in my lifetime, the soothing hot springs of Cascata Del Mulino in Saturnia, Italy would be marvelous. Even a dunk in the glow-in-the-dark ocean on the tiny tropical island Vaadhoo would suffice. And, I know it would be such a temptation to touch those amazing flammable ice bubbles on Alberta's Lake Abraham in Alberta, Canada. If my hearing aids are good to go, the "Taos Hum" in Mexico sounds like a fabulous spot to visit.

By the same token, a more spiritually-oriented escape gleaned from nature's phenomena would also enlighten, renew spirit and refresh the mind. Our universe is a place full of wonder and mysticism to enjoy and add meaning, thought, and purpose to our lives. Sedona, Arizona, for example, is known for energy vortexes and a home of many psychics. That's on our travel list. Glastonburg, England is said to be one of the earth's seven spiritual energy centers with the ley lines of St. Michael and Mary Magdalene crossing over it. I make no secret of my love and devotion to Saint Michael and wonder what vibes and connections I might encounter there.

Many people often experience some sort of psychic phenomena, now and then, but chalk it up as a mere coincidence. Psychic phenomenon is just another experience of God. It's an amazement produced by the invisible powers of the psychic realm and speaks the truth of the universe because this is not only a physical place; but also a metaphysical and spiritual one. (12)

Certain things in this everyday world cannot be understood or explained beyond a reasonable doubt which sometimes causes fear and skepticism. But open-minded individuals graciously see it as normal and accept each remarkable surprise with a "WOW!

Every human is psychic, to some degree, including our pets. But, the psychic is not necessarily the Spiritual. These are two different faculties. Being psychic does not mean that a thread of religion or even a grain of Spirituality is attached. Psychic phenomenon is a paranormal existence which dwells within spirituality—because of its existence of belief, energy, the unknown, and seen/unseen spiritual beings that are of the Spiritual World. (12)

The possibilities of having psychic paranormal experiences are endless. They can happen in any form, anywhere, at anytime, to anybody. They are driven directly by God and His divine beings with purpose through thoughts, voices, laughter, whistles, fragrances, gifts or apports, in dreams and daydreams, by various other kinds of phenomena...or appear visibly through psychic photography. These awe-inspiring instances can be validated by psychic intuition and direct psychic medium communication.

Psychic phenomena has connections to psychic ability and can be seen and experienced through, but not limited to, the numerous ways that follow:

A

Astrology is an ancient system of divination that uses planet, star, and moon positions.

Aura is an energy field or a life force.

C

Channeling is a trance-like state used by psychic mediums to contact spirits.

Clairaudience is the art of hearing voices, music, and sounds that are not audible to the normal ear, and may not be of physical form.

Clairvoyant Mediums is having an ability for extrasensory perception.

Criminology entails using psychics in the investigation of criminal crimes and court cases.

D

De'ja' Vu is the knowledge and perceiving of future events where no control can be exercised over.

Depossession is the act of exorcising attached discarnate human spirits and nonhuman spirits allegedly attached to living people, causing a host of physical, mental, or emotional ills.

E

Empathy is the art of tuning in on an intuitive or psychic level to the emotions, moods, and attitudes of a person.

F

Fortune Telling is the same as having a psychic reading. It is all the great art of divination.

G

Ghost is a term used to describe the spirit of a person who has died.

Graphology is an intuitive psychic reading through the medium of a person's writing.

H

Halo is a ring or circle of radiant light, which crowns the head of deities, holy beings, and saints.

I

Intuition means the ability or an insight to instantly understand a situation in all its dimensions without any conscious effort.

L

Lucid Dreams occur when the dreamer is aware of the fact that they are dreaming.

M

Metaphysics means studying what defies the preconceived laws of physics or nature.

Mysticism is often described as a direct experience of God or a union with God.

N

Near Death Experience is when patients claim that they died and traveled into the light, saw their own body from a distance and observed that they were not in their former body.

New Age represents a movement or wave of new ideas, based upon one's own experiences, acceptance of the old ones with a new rationale, or as reactions to the traditional beliefs and practice.

O

The Occult is now explained as beliefs and practices that are beyond the understanding of ordinary people.

Omens of Jupiter is considered as the 'Prince of Light, Jupiter Optimus Maximus,' and the 'Shepherd of the Stars.' Jupiter could see and provide omens to indicate the future through the flight of birds.

Omens of Saturn of which Saturn is the star of the sun. Its position and its movement around the sun send significant messages in the form of omens.

Ouija Board is a polished board with letters of alphabet inscribed upon it together with the words YES and NO.

Out of Body Experience happens spontaneously and varies from person to person. Many people who have had the experience actually see their body from another point in space.

P

Palmistry is the art of studying the formation of the total hand including the formation of fingers, their characteristics, finger nails, finger prints or impressions, thumb, skin texture, color, the shape, hardness and flexibility, and above all the lines or creases of the palm of the hand.

Paranormal phenomenon is one that is beyond the normal experience and understanding of the ordinary man.

Parapsychology is the study and research in the scientific basis of the various aspects of the psychic phenomena such as the metaphysical, the psi or the psychic, the divination, world of spirits.

Phrenology is reading someone based on the person's physical abnormalities.

Physiognomy is the art and science of reading character from the facial and bodily form.

Predictions are similar to a precognition, but it differs in the fact that the information gathered is obtained through the divine psychic powers of inspiration, psychic gifts, sign reading, or the altering of consciousness, and they concern the individual.

Precognition is the knowledge of the future, and is being able to see things that may happen through special ways.

Premonition is a temporary state of mind that is usually associated with traumatic events such as accidents, or deaths and is usually caused by anxiety, unease, and a gut-level feeling which induces an apprehension of a probable future event.

Prophecy is a divinely inspired vision of great events to happen, which are so important that they have turned thousands and thousands of people to follow them.

PSI is the twenty-third letter of the Greek Alphabet, and used in parapsychology to include extra sensory perception and psycho kinesis.

Psychics refer to the subject of study and practice of extra sensory abilities. In fact these abilities are not just 'extra sensory' in the mundane sense of the words.

Psychic Gifts can surface up or disappear at any time, anywhere, for any reason. The best way to nurture these gifts is to start thinking of them. Keep practicing these gifts by using the tools of the trade such as tarot cards...

Psychic Mediums can convince any skeptic beyond doubt about the existence of the spirits and also his own skill in contacting them. The spirits, in some cases, reveal intimate information about the client seekers, which is known only to them.

Psychic Network is a kind of dynamic and interactive community or a circle of people interested in the subject of psychics. The participants have various degrees of psychic abilities and achievements.

Psychic Visions are not dreams but premonitions that in the near future translate into reality.

Psychokinesis represent mind and motion.

Psychometry is the art of getting impressions or visions from a piece of jewelry or object by simply touching or holding it in your hand.

R

Reincarnation is the process of the soul returning to inhabit a physical form after death.

Retrocognition is the art of seeing or sensing the past. This occurs at spontaneous times, but very uncommonly during the course of daily life, dreams, and parapsychology experiments.

Runes has roots from an ancient Anglo-Saxon word that meant 'secret' or 'mystery.'

S

Scrying is a method of divination done by gazing into a crystal ball or mirror until clairvoyant visions are seen on the surface of the minds eye.

Spirit Guide is a non physical entity that is usually seen as the Higher Self, an angel, a highly evolved being or group mind, or a spirit of the dead.

Spiritualist Medium is a person who can connect him or herself with the spirits, spirit guides, ghosts, and angels. Usually the spiritualist medium inherits this ability to connect and communicate with the spirits from his or her parents and grandparents. 'Mediumism' is a fascinating paranormal phenomenon.

T

Tarot is an ancient form of divination. Tarot means wheel of life. It is a representation or an image of the universe. Tarot is like ordinary playing cards but consists of usually 72 cards.

Tea Leaf Reading is one of the simplest ways of foretelling the future and anyone can learn to master the talent, providing they have the necessary patience.

True Psychic Stories arouse a lot of interest and curiosity among listeners. (12)

SPIRITUAL ORBS

Orbs belong to the paranormal realm. Most people firmly believe and agree that they are physical manifestations connected to the Spirit World. Transitioned loved ones often manifest, or show themselves, as transparent balls of light energy. These spirit-orbs may move fast, slow, zig-zag, hover, or glow. They are seen with our naked eye, not with the third eye. Orbs are commonly noticed in snapshots taken at family celebrations such as reunions, graduations, weddings, or any important event that they would normally have attended if still physically here on Earth. Now, they mingle as energy-balls to offer unique evidence of their attendance and presence among us.

But, not every orb that shows up in photographs is truly of the paranormal kind. How can you tell the difference between fake orbs and authentic spiritual ones? With digital cameras, dust often gets digitized causing 'dust orbs' which often have a thin, faded appearance. A 35 mm camera ensures a greater chance to capture the 'real' ones.

Authentic orbs are brighter, more solid, and some have a trail of light behind the actual orb often seen with multiple edges as if they're moving. When you see a face in one, you may intuitively guess who it could be. If you feel strongly about one, it may be a spirit trying to get your attention. They act through intuition to encourage you to have a visit through a psychic medium. If you ask at a reading, the spirits usually tell who sent it and why. Spirits love it when we look or talk about them in photos for they never want to be forgotten but kept alive in our memories. I have found that they will not release information on the exact meanings of their colors, or how spiritual orbs are actually formed. That information is honored and held as a divine secret that awaits us in the afterlife.

Through iPhone video recordings, my clients have captured clips of orbs in motion as they mingle among guests at private parties, gallery reading, or at anytime the app is on. I especially enjoy the rarities that have rainbow-like effects as those signify to me that the spirit is extremely happy and content. Orbs can appear indoors or outdoors at any time of the day or night around people, pets, or in nature. In my opinion, orb photos need to be carefully analyzed for authenticity and appreciated as inspirational wondrous occurrences.

Unvalidated indoor orb.

A young man's spirit presence at waterfall visit.

A grandfather (green orb) protected motorcyclists from an approaching herd of deer.

Grandmother's spirit appears as a funnel-shaped image.

An uncle (white orb) guides travelers on trip to Kentucky.

People with a fascination for finding peculiar things in the pictures they take are considered psychicphotographers who enjoy psychography. Some individuals seem to be magnets for attracting attention-grabbing images of orbs, angels, apparitions, and other paranormal happenings.

Increasing our chances to capture what's around us and in front of our camera lens may be attributed to the fact that we are all made of energy like those rarities. Energy surrounds us and vibrates at various frequencies. By raising our vibrational energy through our daily habits of spiritual communication, meditation, worship, prayer...we heighten our odds for seeing evidence of paranormal experiences with our own eyes.

Pay attention to loved ones on the Other Side. They send unique signs to make it known that they continue to exist in our lives and want to be included. It's just another of their mystical ways to connect with us and offer spiritual evidence of their supernatural abilities.

Intuitive ability and the paranormal go hand-in-hand. Any person may intuitively connect to the Spirit World while snapping pictures which tends to increase the frequency of unusual images or objects noticed, especially if using a 35 mm camera or a digital one. Viewers are pleasantly surprised by these unexpected paranormal 'showings' that offer a hello, comfort, inspiration, strengthen beliefs, and touch hearts by their evidence that they are with us in our daily lives.

Some individuals are infatuated with 'ghost photography.' They find excitement when ghosts are visibly seen in their photos. Ghosts are simply the souls or spirits of the dead that appear in some form of an apparition or manifestation. They are not typically considered to be our beloved spirits that surround us. They are usually aloof strangers to us, loved by others, or perhaps unloved by all on earth. Paranormal investigators visit various sites including haunted houses, grave sites, and historical landmarks in their quest to find and photograph the existence of these souls.

Loved one sends love through heart clouds.

Face cloud gave beachgoer sense of peace about her mom's recent loss.

Cloud sign sent to spirit's duck-loving brother.

Passenger apparition surprised a biker.

A spirit's photo taken from inside a formal dining room of Civil War historical mansion through a set of French doors. It couldn't be explained except for my feelings I received from the spirit soldier that his purpose was to protect the property. He felt very comfortable being there.

THE HUNT

"Solo, but never alone"

This true story stems from good-spirit humor—a friendly, loving spirit competition over a young lady, Lisa. It began when I drove to her house around 7 P.M. on December 3, 2020. I had departed from Volant, PA after I finished my prior scheduled readings at Wicked Little Witches Gift Shop.

My drive on the rural Route 168 to my destination was peaceful. I always keep the radio off so Spirit can easily connect to me on the way to my appointment. One particular male spirit appeared and rode the entire twenty mile distance to that final appointment of the day. I sensed his quietness but high energy level for the upcoming reading.

When I arrived at the residence, a lighted wreath spread holiday cheer. The gentle spirit-passenger was at my side.

I knocked. A petite, pretty girl in comfy pink sweats opened the door. "Hello! I'm Lisa. Come in out of the cold."

I abstained from my usual handshake—a pandemic safety precaution. Instead, I nodded. "And I'm Greg Nicholas. Pleased to meet you, Lisa."

She extended her arm toward the kitchen table and invited me to help myself to a tray of Stromboli slices. "You're probably hungry." She reached for a beverage. "Would you like iced tea, coffee, soda, or bottled water?"

"Rootbeer, please," I said. While I munched, I laid out my customary items in preparation for the reading. I turned to Lisa. "I have to tell you that a male presence is here with us. He rode in the car with me from Volant."

She reared back. Her brow raised and her face twisted.

"He says he was like a Dad to you, but not by blood. Do you know who he is?"

Her face softened into a wide grin. "It has to be Rod. Not biological, but the best I ever had."

"There's another man coming forward. I sense he's your grandfather." I paused while he explained his message. "He's saying you were like one of his real daughters. You practically lived at his house."

Lisa giggled. "Yeah, that's true. I was always there. They were both great father-figures in my life."

The grandmother pushed to the forefront eager to speak and the two males remained on the sidelines. When I departed for home that evening, I never expected Lisa to call me within days for a needed validation.

On December 8th, I received a private Facebook message to contact Lisa. In that text conversation, she revealed no details. She had one question for the Spirit World. She wanted to know who was with her on the previous Monday afternoon.

I messaged Lisa the answer I received from Spirit. "I'm getting it was both the fellow who rode in the car with me and the grandfather."

"Thank you!" Lisa texted back. "I thought so, I could sense them around me. You won't believe what happened! I'll tell you the whole story when we both have more time to talk in person...."

Lisa later shared her unique journal entry details about the insightful event:

"On Monday, Dec.7th, my husband, Josh, left early in the morning for work. I had errands to run then planned to go hunting in the acreage behind our home.

All morning, I talked aloud to Rod and my Grandpa. I asked that they protect me in the woods and help spook in a deer. After lunch, I fell asleep in front of the television. I woke startled. My intuition told me to hurry into the woods. I panicked because it was after 3:00 P.M. and feared I blew my chances.

I settled into my designated hunting spot, and stilled. A Blue Jay pecked at leaves for seeds and insects. I scanned the field and noticed something brownish in the distance. I wasn't sure what it was but didn't think it had been there before. Wanting to get a closer look, I used the gun's scope to magnify the object. *A deer!* I fired; ejected; quickly reloaded; and pulled the lens to my eye again. *Shit!* Did I miss it? But why didn't it run on that loud bang? *Is it deaf or too scared to move?* Then I saw it in my crosshairs. Even though thoughts flashed like lightning in my head, my finger had instinctively squeezed the trigger. Another thunderous BOOM! Once again, birds darted, bunnies and squirrels scattered—nothing visible in my scope. My knees and arms trembled with excitement and anticipation. I hurried across the field to see if I could find a downed deer.

Thoughts seeped. My intuition told me that I had fired in different directions. But, I knew I stood in approximately the same place. Were they two separate deer? I called my husband and informed him about my confusion and uncertainty in all the excitement. He immediately left work to help me search. He suggested that if I found it, to inspect its hide for two bullet holes.

I ended the call and walked farther. The deer had dropped dead in a patch of clover. Thanks be to God it wasn't in thick jagger bushes or thistles. I inspected its warm, limber body. It had one hole right through the neck. I dug through my backpack for a rope then tied its front legs together for the drag home. When Josh arrived, we both tugged and pulled the carcass. The plan was to get to a clearing near our farmhouse and later load the doe into the bed of the pickup truck.

Halfway there we stopped to catch our breath. It would soon be pitch dark. We needed to speed it up. So, I continued to drag the deer while Josh went back into the woods to scout for a possible blood trail or a second deer. Two shots; two deer? Josh was anxious to see if my intuition was correct. If he couldn't find another one, it would be pure speculation.

This was only my second year of hunting. Josh had skill and experience in tracking. He spotted drops of blood on a thickness of fallen oak leaves. He followed his clues deeper into the timber.

Meanwhile, I had come back into the woods but couldn't set eyes on him. I yelled, "BABE!" several times until I heard his faint echo. "Found her!"

I ran where my instincts led me. My heart pounded, adrenaline pumped. The sun was slipping over the horizon and so was I—on a steep hillside—in greasy mud and muck now freezing with a top coating of patchy ice crystals. When I regained balance, I noticed my husband's safety-orange outfit in among the fat oak trees. He was dragging another deer.

By the time we reached one other, we both needed to catch our breath. Josh grinned. He caught a chill and began to shiver. A glance at my iPhone confirmed temperatures had dipped into the 20's. A light steam rose from the nostrils, mouth, and hide of the serene deer. Those big, beautiful doe eyes stared right through me. I felt deep sadness for shooting her. My thoughts drifted. Is this a normal feeling for empaths, like me, when it comes to wild game?

"I can't believe this," Josh said. "You shot; ejected; reloaded; and shot again thinking it was the same one; but you actually shot two separate deer within seconds and distances of each other. Way to go Anne Oakley!"

I snuggled into Josh's side to get a closer look at my kill—a single bullet wound through the upper chest. Then, I leaned into his arms for some sweet rewards, a kiss and embrace. Creepy noises and darkness settled in. This wasn't the time or place to linger any longer. With iPhone flashlights in one hand and a taut rope in the other, we barely got out of the woods before both phone batteries drained. A glint of moonlight guided us home.

During the drive to the deer processor, I pictured the hunt in my head. Flashbacks of my recent spiritual reading stirred my thoughts. Did Rod and Grandpa show up together again—to hunt with me? I recalled Grandpa's Old Spice cologne being distinct in the air mere moments before the scent of gunpowder. And, it felt like somebody leaned against my shoulder just before the second shot. Rod? In that instant, he came to mind.

Their presence had centered me. In my heart, I 'knew' they assisted in my two successive shots, somehow, by some unimaginable mystical way. Deserved credit belonged to these incredible men and seasoned hunters who both were like 'fathers' to me and continue to be.

I thanked this wonderful duo for the hunt with me and for their continued connections and blessings. I'm proud to remain 'like a daughter' to each."

Over the holidays, Lisa and I bumped into each other in public. She expressed gratitude for the readings and validations. She was grateful to God that He made it possible for us to continue in life after death. As a believer in the Spirit World, Lisa's hunt held a deeper meaning in connections with God and loved ones. She said it gave her much needed comfort, joy, faith, and food for the table during the pandemic. Yes, and a great hunting story with bragger's rights!

Spirit later relayed, in another reading, that Lisa's bagging 'double deer' had indeed been orchestrated by her 'double father figures' from the Spirit World. Lisa hunted solo, but was never alone in the woods.

This true account provides observable evidence that supernatural phenomenon plays out more commonly than most people think, believe, or even recognize.

OUR SENSES

THE THIRD EYE

A human's invisible third eye is related to the sixth sense. It is located in the area between the eyebrows and the hairline, encompassing the forehead and going deep into the center of the brain at the pineal gland. It is thought to be in the center of the forehead or a little lower, right above the eyebrows. It may seem like it fills the entire forehead and encircles the top of the head. You know exactly where it is when you connect to it.

The third eye is important when using intuition. It has no limits of space or time. It allows one to have visions, view things in astral traveling, or details of an out of body experience. It is as unique as a fingerprint and a different experience for each individual. I don't actually see mine open but know it does when I'm using it.

SUE'S SIXTH SENSE

Everybody has a sixth sense to some degree or another. Call it extrasensory perception, intuition, a gut-feeling, or a hunch that goes beyond the basic five senses. Some individuals recognize and tune into it while others are oblivious.

This is a story from a client, Sue, who was left baffled until she later learned she had the ability of 'clear knowing' or claircognizance.

It began one day, when this grandmother-to-be received the call. The pregnant daughter-in-law was on her way to the hospital to deliver a precious bundle of joy.

Sue and others rushed to the occasion and gathered in a nearby hospital waiting area. News came that the mother was fine except that all the blood vessels in her face were broken from the strain of her forceful birthing pushes. But, as for the newborn, he was in serious distress and had been rushed into emergency exploratory surgery due to a heart problem. Loved ones gasped, choked up, or shed tears. Heads drooped as people texted the news.

Sue wholeheartedly began to pray. Spontaneously, a thought appeared out of nowhere and flashed through her mind. Without thinking, she repeated it aloud. "Two stitches and that's it!" Family members glared at her and turned their heads. Sue, confused, sat isolated among the whisperers and snivelers.

The surgeon finally arrived to update the status of the infant. He explained that they had found a small tumor on the newborn's heart. His face beamed. "But, I don't expect any future complications. I removed it. He only needed two stitches. That's it."

"When can we see him?" someone asked.

The doctor grinned. "Recovery room nurses should be taking him to the nursery shortly."

Individuals expressed gratitude to God and the doctor while a few stunned relatives questioned Sue.

"How did you know that?"

She shrugged her shoulders. "I'm not sure." Sue steepled her hands together. "It popped into my thoughts. Perhaps from God or the Holy Spirit."

Sue's niece shifted position in her chair. "I don't understand. Is that possible?"

"How else would I have ever known that?" Sue said.

The group quieted with flat gazes in relief and disbelief.

The proud new father broke the silence."Well, thanks be to Him for answered prayers. I'm so happy!" He leaned in and embraced Sue. One by one each stood to congratulate the proud papa.

"Let's take a peek through the nursery window at this little blessing!" Sue said. "Follow me."

THE CLAIR SENSES

What has become known as the eight 'clair' or 'clear' psychic senses are the basics of intuitive development. (13) Every human is born with intuition. It can be enhanced and fine-tuned depending on a person's awareness, experiences, and spiritual growth.

I was not raised in the days of modern technology or with the 'clair senses.' There was nothing beyond what my mother taught me. It was simple old school basics of what Mom knew about psychic seeing, hearing, knowing, tasting,smelling, feeling, and sensing. The rest, I learned after I left home when I conversed with other mediums and became interested in new concepts and terminology.

Over time, information and awareness of the psychic world and the psychic self became available and popular.

- CLAIRVOYANCE means 'clear seeing' or the intuitive ability to see visions beyond what the normal eye can see, without using the eyes. It's an intuitive knowledge of perceiving people and things from the spiritual realm within the mind's eye—known as 'the third eye,' located in the middle of the forehead. Clairvoyants can see colors, symbols, shapes, scenes...and some are artists that draw what they perceive. Some individuals may only see shadows out of the corner of their eye, a flash of unexplainable light, or a full apparition. These people may be drawn to being psychic mediums, counselors, or police investigators.

• Claircognizance is a 'clear knowing' without a shadow of a doubt, about people or events that you normally would have no possible way to ever know it. It may be a hunch, that's always right, that someone needs help or something is about to happen. This is linked to faith and divine guidance. It is one's following strong gut-instincts. It comes as a sudden flash of knowledge and a sense of 'knowing.'

• Clairaudience is 'clear hearing' based on sounds in the mind beyond what we normally hear. Someone may call your name, whisper, talk, hum, or even sing when no one is present. You could hear a bang, a knock, or a door open or close with no explanation. People accustomed to this well-known ability have learned to focus on messages received and trust the voices. These intuitives are often musicians, dancers, singers, speakers, and writers.

• Clairempathy means an empath can 'clearly sense' the emotions and feelings of others beyond normal capabilities. This is one who can clearly perceive the mental or emotional states of others. It's natural for an empathic person to absorb what they sense, and take it in to help another release mirrored feelings. If they visited after a husband and wife argument, they would be able to sense the anger and hurt in the room.

• Clairsentience or a clairsentient person can 'clearly experience' the emotions and feelings of others. They don't just sense it, but get a physical sensation in their body in which they 'feel the experience' of other people's emotions, ailments, or injuries. They tend to be more sensitive to a deliberate 'touch' or 'brush' from spirit-beings and get more goosebumps and body tingles when beloved ones are near. Those with this ability have inclinations to become nurses, healers, therapists, mentors, teachers, detectives, motivational speakers, and compassionate friends.

• Clairtangency is 'clear touching' or an intuitive sense of touch used to gain interpretation of an inanimate object's energy. It's also known as psychometry whereby one's touch garnishes information about the object's history and owners in the past or present.

• Clairsalience and clairalience both mean 'clear smelling' and picking up scents beyond what is in the physical world. It may be a spontaneous, fleeting smell of a certain cigar brand, kitchen spice, tea, flower, or a favorite perfume...of a deceased loved one which instantly triggers a reminder or memory with that sign of their presence.

• Clairgustance refers to 'clear tasting' or the ability to taste from the spiritual realm that associated with a specific person, place, or thing without ever putting anything in the mouth. It can be connected to past, present, or future taste. (13)

In regards to clairgustance, one client asked me to verify her father's favorite cookie. I suddenly had a strong smell and taste of fresh oranges. Her jaw dropped when I replied, "orange-drop cookies."

During one reading, a male client complained of stomach pains which grew worse during the sitting. I sensed a foul, weird, undetectable taste. I suggested he get to Urgent Care. The next day, he revealed he had been diagnosed with food poisoning.

A young female suspected the step-father in the murder of her mom. I immediately got a mental image of a neon-orange bottle. For a fleeting moment, I felt deathly ill with insatiable body pain and nausea accompanied by a chemical taste. My senses gave insight of a poisoning. After the daughter conducted a private investigation, she found the smoking gun in the garage cupboard. Test results determined it to be an illegal possession of an agent of mass destruction known as Agent Orange. She was slated to be his next victim.

Personally, I find clairtangency 'unclear' in regards to being a unique clair sense. To me, inanimate objects, alone, don't surrender enough clear, accurate, adequate information for authentication and validation in the absence of other senses. I use psychometry as a tool in conjunction with my mediumistic ability of direct communication with the Spirit World to produce a richer reading for clients in regards to objects.

INTUITIVES

Psychic work and intuitive work happen on much the same level, but with fundamental differences. Psychics must 'process' or 'translate' their insight into real-life meaning. (14)

Intuitives tend to get flashes of insight or intuition that need no translation. It tends to come from out of the blue similar to what is known as 'mother's intuition.' We all are born with intuition and most people experience it all the time. It feels and sounds like our own thoughts because it is. Images or thoughts which instantly pop into the mind are usually intuitive messages. (14)

Intuition is a spiritual safety net that grows more clear the more it is honored and followed. Words of gratitude after every intuitive flash ensures more frequency and clarity. Think of it as a muscle–the more it's flexed and massaged, the stronger and clearer intuitiveness becomes. (14)

Professional intuitives are best reserved for personal revelation, insight, and circumstances that affect life, love, relationships, and journeys." (14)

The Four Clairs of Intuition and Psychic Ability

Clairvoyance, clairaudience, clairsentience, and claircognizance are the four main avenues our intuition uses to communicate with us. (15) These are psychic faculties or modalities. When an individual can determine which one is the dominant faculty, that clair sense can be strengthened, developed, and utilized to increase one's own intuitive potential and psychic abilities. With patience and nurturing, intuition can grow and blossom over time. (16)

LIST OF PSYCHIC ABILITIES

Psychics are people with an ability to gather information through the psychic senses. They use their spiritual senses to gain insight into people, events, and situations. Logic is needed to process and translate any data received in order to decipher words, feelings, images, and symbols in a way that makes sense. (17)

- Apportation-The ability to undergo materialization, disappearance or teleportation of an object.
- Astral projection or mental projection-The ability to voluntarily project the astral body (consciousness), being associated with the out-of-body experience, in which the astral body is felt to temporarily separate from the physical body.
- Automatic writing-The ability to draw or write without conscious intent.
- Divination-The ability to gain insight into a situation using occult means.
- Dowsing-The ability to locate water, sometimes using a tool called a dowsing rod.
- Energy medicine-The ability to heal with one's own empathic, etheric, astral, mental or spiritual energy.
- Levitation or transvection- The ability to float or fly by mystical means.
- Mediumship or channeling-The ability to communicate with spirits.
- Precognition or telekinesis-The ability to perceive future events.

• Psychic surgery-The ability to remove disease or disorder within or over the body tissue via an "energetic" incision that heals immediately afterwards.

• Psychokinesis or telekinesis-The ability to manipulate objects with one's mind.

• Psychometry or psychoscopy-The ability to obtain information about a person or an object by touch.

• Pyrokinesis-The ability to control flames, fire, or heat using one's mind.

• Remote viewing, telesthesia or remote sensing-The ability to see a distant or unseen target using extrasensory perception.

• Telepathy-The ability to transmit or receive thought supernaturally.

DOMESTIC VIOLENCE

Abuse is not love. It is one person in a relationship having power and control over the other person.

It takes many forms: physical, verbal, emotional, economic, stalking and harassment, and sexual.

Anyone can be a victim of domestic abuse, regardless of age, race, gender, sexual orientation, faith, class, or education.

No one deserves to be abused. The abuse is not one's fault. Victims are not alone during the abuse nor is it ever kept a secret. As a psychic medium, I can attest to that statement. Abusive situations are actively observed by the Spirit World, as in the case of Lillian.

THE BATTERED WIFE

The 2021 new year had just arrived. With it, a new client darted into a corner shop in downtown Struthers, Ohio for a scheduled psychic medium reading. The lanky lady, in her thirties, was a plain-Jane, wearing no make-up, pretentious clothing, or hair style. The first thing I noticed was a blackened eye, facial cuts, and shaky hands that fumbled to set a purse and phone on the table. Her torso squirmed in the chair as she bounced her crossed legs.

I introduced myself and she reciprocated with the name, Lillian. Several spirits appeared around this 'Nervous Nelly.'

"An older woman is here," I said. "Were you on the couch today watching cooking shows?"

"Yeah."

"She's showing me a cover, or blanket. Was that hand made?"

Lillian nodded.

"Do you remember who made it?"

Her face brightened. "My mother-in-law."

"She says she's been with you all day. Did you flinch when she touched your face?"

"Oh my! Was that her?" She giggled. "It felt like a spider."

I chuckled. "There's been a man with a long beard standing here beside her. His voice is very deep and raspy. Who's a disappointment? He keeps saying, 'He's such a disappointment.'"

At that, Lillian dropped her head and doubled over bawling. Her hands cupped her knees as she gently rocked back and forth. I didn't quite get what that was all about until the mother-in-law relayed, "We didn't raise our son to abuse any living thing, especially her!"

The male-spirit chimed in. "We know and support her thoughts of leaving him. That's her decision."

I communicated their messages to my client.

Lillian's head lifted slightly. She dabbed at her eyes. "It's so embarrassing."

I countered. "I hear the spirits tell-all everyday. They're concerned and want to send you clarity and love."

Her eyes leveled with mine. "My in-laws are so amazing." She paused. "They 'knew' I needed someone to turn to. Things have gotten worse since they both recently died from COVID-19. That's when 'he' started taking all his anger out on me—like it's all my fault."

She glanced at her watch, stood, and picked up her belongings in a tizzy. "I need to hurry before he's home and in a rage. I've been gone way too long."

"I hope this reading helped," I said.

"It did."

Lillian stepped forward toward the door and stopped. She abruptly turned around, "Maybe I need to bring him for a reading to talk to his parents."

I nodded. "Might be worth a try. Sounds like he's not dealing well with life or death. Call anytime."

Her body pivoted and she hurried on her way.

I Don't Want To Talk To Him

I had traveled to West Virginia for a day of scheduled readings at a house party. A fidgety lady, in her forties, sat down. She picked at her fingernails and her toes tapped against the floor.

I greeted her and introduced myself. She kept her head lowered and chipped away at her nail polish. "What's your name?"

"Elaine."

"Have you had a reading before?"

"No," she shyly replied. "My friend talked me into it."

"Well, a woman who says she's your grandmother is present and says 'hello.' She talks about how she raised you."

Elaine looked at me. She nodded and smiled. All at once, my left arm hurt. The grandmother said to me, "He's here!" and stepped back as a grandfather figure appeared. I relayed that to Elaine.

Her eyes widened. She stiffened in her chair and flinched. "I don't want to talk to him!"

"Why is he saying he's sorry?"

Elaine's voice warbled. "I can't." She paused. She squeezed her eyes shut. "I don't want to hear that—or anything from him." She buried her face in her hands.

147

I broke my connection with him and sat in silence. It was rare that clients had such strong, negative reactions to a spirit during a reading. I sensed her pain in my thumping left arm.

Suddenly, Elaine looked up. Her words rang true. "It's a little too late for apologies. When I was sixteen, I was late coming home from school. Gramps had a terrible temper. He didn't give me a chance to explain. In a rage, he grabbed me by my hair with one hand and with the other he twisted my left arm behind my back. I heard a pop, a snap. It was so painful I thought it broke. Grandma took me to the hospital. Turned out as a fracture. I wore a brace for weeks. It's difficult for me to forgive him to this day. From time to time, I still have bad dreams of him hurting me."

The grandmother reappeared. "Things were never the same after he snapped her arm. They both need to forgive and be forgiven. He can't hurt her anymore."

I made that message known to Elaine.

"What he did still hurts every time I hear his name or remember," she said. "Why should I forgive? He doesn't deserve it."

I heard my own mother's voice echo in my head when I offered her words to my client. "God blesses true forgiveness which heals all wounds."

Elaine slowly shook her head in agreement, but without emotion.

"Your grandma wants to talk about that adorable great-granddaughter she never got to hold...."

We were over that hiccup. The reading proceeded with positivity for Elaine's path and journey in life.

When Catherine sat down at my table for her reading, I felt a strong female presence and anxiety. I told my client that the lady coming through felt like her mother. "Her death was very recent?"

Catherine silently counted on three fingers.

I knew it was fresh, just months ago. "Oh, I'm getting a sensation of being pushed and slapped hard in my face!"

"That's Mom!"

"It is," I relayed. "'I'm sorry,' she says. 'I'm so sorry!'"

My client straightened. With a stern expression, she made apologies for the slap I felt. "In Mom's last year of life she became physically abusive to me. I couldn't hit her back, but yelled at her to stop."

I clearly understood Catherine's situation. But, now, her mother was on the Other Side and very sincere in her apology for abusiveness. The spirits showed a childhood version of Catherine's mother who was abused similarly by her parents. During the final months of life, confused and unaware of her actions because of Alzheimer's, she reverted back to childhood in a role-reversal and inflicted abuse on her own daughter.

Catherine leaned forward and touched my hand. "I'm relieved that Mom came through with an apology. I never would have been able to forgive Mom had we not figured this out today."

"There's no dementia in the afterlife," I said. "Her faculties are lucid; her apologies sincere."

THIRD PARTY PAIN

During a house party in Cleveland, a sitter's father came through. I relayed to the son that I faintly heard two words, backhand and rake. Suddenly, a stabbing pain spiked in the middle of my back. My body stiffened. My eyes squeezed shut as it quickly reoccurred then vanished.

The son winced. "Are you okay man?"

"It didn't last long," I said. "It's an empathetic pain. It's common for me to feel the hurt, pain, and anxiety of others during a reading. It's part of the spirit communication."

"Man, I can't imagine," the client said. "I thought mine was bad enough. Dad often backhanded me when I was a teen. On occasion, he would break a rake or thick yardstick over my back."

I shifted in my chair. "I felt it."

The client cringed, his eyes bulged.

"Your father sends his apologies for being too strong-armed with you. He asks for forgiveness."

"It's all in the past now," he sighed. "I forgive him."

AT AGE SEVEN

My Mom's sister and husband came to visit one weekend. My cousin, Ron, came along. I thought he was so cool because he was 14. My brother, John, was 13 years older than I but had gone away to college. We lived in a small modest home in Oil City, Pennsylvania. That meant that it was proper for my aunt and uncle, as guests, to have my bedroom for the duration of their stay. I was raised to respect my elders so there was no fussing or fuming about it.

Ron and I made a tent over the couch, like we did every time they visited. We had fun 'camping out' in the living room. We turned off the lights and used our flashlights to read spooky ghost stories, tell jokes, and eat junk food late into the night. We both drifted to sleep without even brushing our teeth.

Toward morning, I woke up startled and scared. At age seven, I had never heard the story about the 'birds and the bees' or even knew sex existed. I froze as I felt my cousin's hands grope their way inside my underwear and fondle my privates. Unaware of what he was doing to me, I sensed it was wrong for him to touch me like that. I began to kick, punch, wrestle, and war hoop like a little Indian.

My mother ran into the room, shushing us to not wake up the entire house. She put cartoons on the television to keep us quiet and entertained. She made a pot of coffee and sat near us to read the newspaper before everybody would be awake and expect breakfast. I glared at Ron and watched "Bugs Bunny."

Later that afternoon, our three visitors needed to cut their stay short to attend an outing closer to home. When they were out of sight, I told Mom and Dad what my cousin had done to me that morning. My parents explained that Ron's behavior was morally wrong and unacceptable. Then they called my aunt. They were no longer welcome to stay the night again if Ron was in their company. We prayed that God would guide my cousin on a path of righteousness.

Had it not been for my confession and Mom nipping things in the bud, who knows what might have transpired. Yes, call me out for being a tattle tale, a squealer, a snitch, but Ron learned lessons from the consequences and guidance he received. To my knowledge, he never grew up gay, a rapist, or a sexual abuser. I have chalked it up to natural boyhood curiosity, puberty, and hormones.

Whenever sexual assault victims are brought to light during a reading, I cringe, and think about the "what ifs." My body tenses. But, the personal experience has made me more aware, understanding, and compassionate of both victims and abusers.

Just as our society frowns upon abuse, those in the Spirit World do too. I have had numerous spirits come through to serve as advocates for abused loved ones. I find that deceased abusers often ask the victimized for forgiveness as part of their soul progression in the afterlife.

If you feel you or a loved one suffers from domestic abuse, become familiar with the lists of warning signs. Seek help through local police or domestic abuse agencies and hotlines. The National Domestic Violence Hotline number is 1-800-799-SAFE.

AGE OF AQUARIUS

The "dawn of the Aquarius" is commonly referred to the New Age way of thinking. It had first caught my attention when a client asked me if I was an 'Aquarian' or 'New Ager.' Her question stumped me for my lack of knowledge. Even though I'm an old world medium, I recognized the need to keep up with the times. I had found myself working with an increased number of clients who had latched onto more modernistic beliefs and ideas which aroused a personal investigation.

Astrologers believe that our current astrological age affects humanity, possibly by influences on cultural tendencies. Many see it as a time when humanity takes control of earth and its own destiny as its rightful heritage, with revelation of truth and expansion of consciousness alongside other schools of thought. (18)

Not all astrologers are in agreement on when the Aquarian age exactly started. Some think that it is either an ongoing current age or perhaps a forthcoming astrological age, depending on the method of calculation. Astrological ages are taken to be associated with the procession of the equinoxes. Roughly every 2,150 years the sun's position, at the time of the vernal equinox, will have moved into a new zodiacal constellation. (18)

There are various methods of calculation. In sun-sign astrology, the first sign is Aries, followed by Taurus, Gemini, Cancer, Leo, Virgo, Libra, Scorpio, Sagittarius, Capricorn, Aquarius, and Pisces, whereupon the cycle returns to Aries and through the zodiac signs again which proceed in the opposite direction. Therefore, the Age of Aquarius follows the Age of Pisces. (18)

We are almost out of the Pisces age. We started into the Aquarius age about one hundred years ago. It gradually takes about 200 to 300 years to go from one age to another. (19)

The music festival commonly known as Woodstock was billed as "An Aquarian Exposition" which popularized the heyday of the hippie and New Age Movement in the 1960s and 1970s. (18)

Hair, a 1967 musical, opened with the song "Aquarius." Its first line, "This is the dawning of the Age of Aquarius," brought the Aquarian Age concept to the attention of audiences worldwide. The lyrics were denounced by critics as poetic license which people took literally. (18)

Ultimately, the age of Aquarius' goal for humanity is individual freedom and free will. Advances in science and technology opened the doors of possibilities. We have experienced innovations in 'smart' phones, homes, cars, and televisions. Computers, email, Facebook, internet, blogs, Zoom conferences, and work-from-home options have become a way of life. In addition, drones, commercial space travel, holograms, updates in religion...contribute to global freedom. Society now has the tools and means to realize their wishes and dreams—to have freedom to work what they love, to love who they want, to live wherever they want. Freedom, freedom, and more freedom gained by constant learning. (19)

Aquarius' symbol is the Water Bearer. In reality, it's not water. It represents knowledge poured into a well for all to partake of, regardless of race, religion, or gender. (20)

The Aquarian Age is governed by Uranus, the planet of shocking and revolutionary change and is associated with new freedoms, social justice, and new technology. (21) I realized that our world already has been seeing and experiencing the signs, transitions, and makings of the New Age ways—The Age of Aquarius.

ANDROGENY AND THE AQUARIAN AGE

Uranus governs radical behavior and rebellion against the status quo to accept lifestyles that don't fit into the rigid social norms. (22) As we transition into the Aquarian Age, it's not surprising that gender roles blur and homosexuality becomes more openly accepted. Our planets inspire us to live a life that is authentically true to ourselves. (22)

The term 'Uranian' describes any person that has a desire to move past old ways of thinking and show that by their thoughts and behaviors that they live life uninfluenced by gender issues. But a strong Uranian in a birth chart does not tend to indicate a person will express homosexuality. (22)

Uranian, a nineteenth century term, referred to a person of a 'third sex'—someone with 'a female psyche in a male body' who is sexually attracted to men, and later extended to cover homosexual gender variant females, and a number of other sexual types. (22) This term originated with a transgender scholar, Karl Heinrich Ulrich. (22)

Androgyny is nothing new. Many individuals identify with a partly male, partly female, or indeterminate sex. (18) This is only the beginning of what's to come. The more radical societal changes become, the stronger the backlash of conservatives who fear this kind of extreme alteration to their world view. This is what we will be seeing as Uranus takes us deeper into the Aquarian Age. (18) The conflict becomes more obvious each time I pick up the newspaper or watch a news segment.

The term 'new age' has become popular over the last 60 years. It is a very broad term that is identified by alternative ideas that differ from mainstream Western culture and traditions. (23)

During the 1970's, a range of spiritual or religious beliefs and practices grew. Precise scholarly definitions of this New Age differ in their emphasis, largely as a result of its highly eclectic structure. (23) Although analytically considered to be religious, the designation of 'mind, body, and spirit' is preferred. (23)

"An increased number of people have turned to various unconventional spiritual and therapeutic practices. This New Age Movement is probably best characterized as a 'spiritual supermarket' from which individuals are free to pick and mix those spiritual beliefs and practices which they feel best help them achieve peace of mind or realize their full human potential. New Age pursuits include spirituality, metaphysics, holistic health, and humanitarianism." (23)

"With Spiritualism came the notion of spiritual progress after death and the role of mediums in contacting the Spirit World. Even if some New Agers did not personally adopt it due to a lack of scientific proof or because of religious reasons, they did embrace the underlying idea. They believed in channeling non-physical humans to receive spiritual truths." (23)

Many focused on alternative scientific systems and natural or spiritual healing while alternative medical practices like acupuncture, chiropractic adjustment, natural foods, and herbal remedies grew more common. (23)

"The New Age Movement is not itself a religion. There is no centralized leadership or formal organization and New Agers are not required to hold any particular creedal or doctrinal beliefs. Rather, it is comprised of individuals and groups who share a similar life philosophy and worldview. Generally focused on personal spiritual transformation, New Agers endeavor to usher into the world—a new era of harmony and enlightenment, an era of love and light. It's seen as a vision of a coming era defined by the transformation of our broken society—characterized by poverty, war, racism, etc.—into a united community of abundance, peace, and brotherly love." (24)

"They reject the traditional monotheistic belief in one all-powerful God. Instead, they embrace a monism or the belief that everything is one—and pantheism or the belief that God is everywhere. In fact, when it comes to God, New Agers believe that the self is the seat of the divine. That is, there is a god-aspect within each of us—a tiny sliver of God in every person." (24)

"Moreover, everyone has a responsibility to develop his or her own god-aspect. New Agers encourage individual human evolution to increase awareness of this divine nature. This does not refer to biological evolution, but rather spiritual evolution—a progressive awareness of the self as divine. This need for and possibility of personal transformation is a foundational part of the movement." (24)

"New Age beliefs include the idea that the spiritual realm is responsible for much of what we see and experience in the physical world, as well as the notion that the development of one's own innate divinity will lead to global transformation and world harmony. Belief in psychics, reincarnation, the ability to access the spiritual realm, spiritual explanations for physical suffering, and the presence of spiritual energy in physical objects like mountains or trees are also common ground." (24)

"Practices involve contacting the Spirit World and accessing spiritual dimension, often through altered consciousness. This includes channeling, crystal work, tarot card readings, astrology, and various forms of spiritual healing." (24)

"Humanistic practices are those focused on self-sufficiency, self-improvement, and the development of the god-element within the self. Some examples are yoga, meditation strategies, studying New Age texts, creating a positive environment, concern and volunteer efforts for human need, and for communing with nature." (24)

"Over the past few decades, some New Age ideas have been adopted commonly by mainstream culture among both religious and nonreligious Americans. While yoga and meditation are not exclusively New Age practices, their popularity and prevalence correlate with New Age influence. Eckhart Tolle's A New Earth: Awakening to Your Life's Purpose, promoted by Oprah Winfrey, became a best seller, and the use of alternative medicine dramatically increased over the past few decades." (23)

"The New Age has become the epoch of belief in the spiritual meaning of the Scriptures. Biblical criticism became destructive and had to do with a weakening of the faith still apparent among us.

Undertaking to explain how the Bible came into being, with the variations and errors of texts, the imperfections of language, the conflict of opinion due to the fact that the books of which the Bible consists were brought together by other hands long after the supposed writers flourished, contributed to a new wave of thinking." (24)

The New Agers began as a push-back against authority and the church. They fought for the right to experience various beliefs and make their own decisions. For their own good and longevity, churches were forced to catch up with the times.

"A recent example of this happened when the Catholic Church changed its stance in approval and support of psychic gifts. The Vatican released an official document that addressed the public shift in perspective that spanned the approximate prior 600 years. Parishioners with 'gifts' such as healing, prophecy, and discernment finally became welcomed with open arms." (25)

"People grew eager and energized with evidence that humans survived death, that a spirit could return and establish its identity. New Age assured what which is spiritual must be discerned spiritually, put emphasis on conduct, eternal life, brotherhood, peace, and humanity. New Agers became filled with hope for the transformation of society and the planet." (24)

"The New Age Movement, after all, grew as an extension of history from the similar New Thought Movement of decades prior. Devotees of that movement, also, began to freely interpret the Bible for themselves. They needed a spiritual science of interpretation to offset the destructive work of some churches which people formerly accepted without knowing what to believe." (24)

SHAPING OF THE NEW AGE MOVEMENT

"Additionally, the New Age Movement grew its roots from the past through various influences such as Hinduism, Gnosticism, occultism, and especially nineteenth-century metaphysical religions of New Thought, Spiritualism, Theosophy, and the Human Potential Movement." (24)

"This new movement embraced the Human Potential Movement's belief that human potential has been limited by society. People must experience spiritual healing and growth in order to remedy this, develop their full potential, and live meaningful lives." (24)

"The New Thought Movement, also known as Higher Thought, started in the 1830s in the United States and England as a spiritual movement with roots in metaphysical beliefs. It empowered the birth of New Agers. It helped people achieve a better understanding of divine mysteries, through the power of their thoughts. There was also a movement and philosophy in foreign lands which declared the dead were here, in spirit. Astral plane studies emerged and the notion that the world sprung from spiritual sources. Earthly experiences were recognized for the benefit of spiritual beings." (26)

"New Thought was considered to have been derived, in part, from the unpublished writings of Phineas Quimby. His principles relied more exclusively on spiritual healing than does the New Age Movement. It concentrated on the power of the mind to heal and prosper in a world in which all was mind. New Age extends this healing, share in many interests, beliefs, and practices, yet continues to belong to mainstream Christianity or other religions." (26)

"Quimby believed the real cure to self-healing was in the discovery of our real inner nature as recipients of the divine life. A theory of an essentially spiritual cure starts with the principle that there is but one source of life which emanates from this one living God, and is communicated to all, and communicable to others through us. The remedy for all our ills is at hand. God alone heals." (26)

"He quoted: 'Make the heart of something outside your own being to leap for joy. Attune your soul in harmony with the Divine Life. Live to love, and then you will delight to live; and health will glow and thrill in every organic structure. Find someone whose condition is unhappily like your own. Lift up your hand and your heart, and pull down a blessing upon his head....Be, like Jesus, every one's friend. Seek to make everybody and everything happy...Get well by curing others. Impart life, communicate from your own stock of vital force to others, and life from God.'" (26)

"His teachings were nothing less than 'a new revelation of Christianity.' He saw that for hundreds of years the world had been deprived of an important portion of the gospel of Christ. He believed that mankind needed the truth. There was a new urge in the souls of men toward a new and better humanity built on the principles of Christ. And, never had there been a greater demonstration of the presence of God in the affairs of man. In short, Quimby touted New Thought as an 'influence' not an 'institution.'" (26)

New Agers have entered an optimistic new age, but, the New Thought or Higher Thought Movement pioneers, among others, will always be the original mainstay ingredients in its historical and spiritual smorgasbord.

NEW AGE SPIRITUALITY

Paraphrasing would do no justice to the compilation of researched facts and thoughts in this original piece of writing from God Ministries without serving to confuse and cause misinformation to readers. Therefore it stands, in tack, unadulterated, for the true intent of the educational information and knowledge it provides readers to gain a clear, authentic comprehension of New Age Spirituality.

New Age is a compilation of metaphysical, Eastern-influenced thought systems. These thought systems unite theology, nature, and philosophy. This movement comprises countless "theologies" that often center on religious tolerance and moral diversity. The main phrases (or "isms") that reveal the focal point of New Age thought are "feel-goodism" (do whatever feels good, as long as you are not hurting someone else), "moral relativism" (situational ethics), and "pluralism" (universal tolerance).

The phrase "New Age" refers to the "Aquarian Age" which, according to New Age supporters, is now beginning. This Age is expected to bring peace and enlightenment, as well as reunite humans with "god." New Age doctrine says that humans are currently estranged from god due to a lack of insight concerning god's real nature and reality. In New Age understanding, mankind is central. Humans are considered to be divine, as co-creators, and as the ultimate hope for the future of the world.

Although New Age is generally tolerant of almost any world religion or philosophy, it is opposed to the "narrow-mindedness" of Christianity that teaches Jesus Christ is the only way to eternal salvation.

Christians believe we have all sinned and deserve God's judgment. God, the Father, sent His only Son to satisfy that judgment for those who believe in Him. The creator, Jesus, eternal Son of God, lived a sinless life. He loves us so much that He died for our sins, taking the punishment that we deserve, was buried, and rose from the dead. If you truly believe and trust this in your heart, receiving Jesus alone as your Savior, declaring "Jesus is Lord," you will be saved from judgment and spend eternity with God in heaven.

New Age philosophy is complicated to define because there is no centralized hierarchy, doctrine, or membership. At its foundation, the New Age movement is a religious system with two main doctrines: Evolutionary Godhood and Global Unity.

New Age: The Doctrine of Evolutionary Godhood

Generally, New Age thought supports the theory of organic evolution, but extends the concept to the evolution of the spirit. This is the concept of "Evolutionary Godhood," where the next step in evolution won't be physical, but spiritual. The principles of evolution are constantly moving mankind toward god-consciousness, where man and reality connect in unified enlightenment. The "fittest" already understand this reality, while the "unfit" (such as Christians and other proponents of dogmatic worldviews) act as a hindrance to evolutionary forces.

Many New Age practices are designed to accelerate the evolutionary push into the spiritual realms. These practices include: (i) astral projection, which is training your soul to leave your body and travel around; (ii) channeling spirits, so they may speak through you or guide you; (iii) crystal usage, which purifies the energy systems of your body and mind; and (iv) visualization techniques, which include everything from basic mental imagery to role playing of animals or divine creatures.

In a nutshell, Evolutionary Godhood means that mankind will soon see itself as god. This is often referred to as the "Christ principle" or "Christ consciousness." New Age teaches that we are basically good and inherently divine, and ultimately, we can create our own reality.

New Age: The Doctrine of Global Unity

The second major doctrine of the New Age movement is "Global Unity." This concept typically consists of three parts:

Man Unified With Man

One New Age principle is that we will all realize our proper divine relationship with one another and achieve pure harmony through the acceptance of this divine knowledge. With relational harmony comes economic unity. With economic unity, we can achieve political unity (a single world government) and spiritual unity (a one world religion).

MAN UNIFIED WITH NATURE

Another New Age principle is that god is everything, and everything is god. Therefore, nature is also part of god. We must be in harmony with nature. We must nurture it and be nurtured by it. Mankind is no different than any other animal. We must live in harmony with them, understand them, and learn from them. Actually, many in the New Age movement refer to the union of earth and nature as "Gaia." Gaia is revered, respected, and even worshiped as a god by some. American Indian rituals are also popular in the New Age movement because they focus on the elements of nature and man's relationship to them.

MAN UNIFIED WITH GOD

Since man is divine by nature, all people can realize their "divinity" and contribute to the unified purpose of man, earth and nature. The ultimate goal in life is to fully realize our own divine goodness. The New Age god is impersonal and omnipresent. He (it) has not revealed himself (itself) to mankind, and therefore, mankind is not accountable to any notions of moral law or absolute truth. There is no objective morality in the New Age philosophy. We should have tolerance for all systems of truth, meaning and purpose. We should create a world of pure relativism, where morality and religion are strictly relative to each person's individual notion of reality itself. (27)

RULA'S STRUGGLE

Sunshine beamed through the large open windows of an Ohio shop that spring day. I glanced at my roster of scheduled readings. Rula, was my next client. Within minutes, she darted over the threshold, dropped into the plush chair and adjusted her face mask. It was during the global pandemic so we refrained from any customary handshake when we introduced ourselves. We followed the protocol and kept six feet apart. There were no vaccinations available at that time.

An older male spirit hovered around us. He was ready to talk.

"I'm picking up on a gentleman—a grandfatherly figure. I'm getting his name is Oscar?"

She nodded.

"I'm sensing his death was recent as he's showing me a number two and clutching his chest. Was his passing from a sudden heart attack?

"Yes. A couple months ago."

"Oscar wants you to follow 'your heart.' He walks beside you on this new path. 'Stay strong,' he says. Do you understand that?"

Rula's lips pressed together in a slight grimace. "I think so."

"Your grandfather says that he now gets the picture, but your mother doesn't. He's showing her being very agitated and pointing to the front door screaming, "Go!" He tells me that she has a highfalutin holier than thou attitude."

She nodded and juked her shoulders. "Always."

"Oscar says you recently 'came out.' He's proud of your strength and courage. You're on the right path now."

Rula's words tumbled from her mouth. "I kept it hidden too long. I grew up with pressure–church, people set in their ways. Mom found my suicide note I was working on and sent me away for help. There, I met a girl, just like me." Rula blushed. "She loves me. Life is now worth living. Her family's so understanding and supportive. They accept that God made us this way. We often joke—what if God was gay?"

A female spirit stepped up beside Oscar. She identified herself being his sister. I imparted that to Rula.

"Oh my! Great-Aunt Sophie," Rula said.

Intrigued by what Sophie revealed to me, I locked eyes with Rula. Your aunt tells me she shared a deathbed confession with you.

Rula nodded.

"Seems like you both shared the same secret."

Fat teardrops rolled out when Rula closed her eyes. "But she didn't get a chance to live freely and face her reality or dreams."

"Your aunt laughs. She says, 'Maybe in my next life.'"

Rula turned her head. She gave me the side-eye. Her voice was stern. "Do you believe we really get second chances?"

My response to Rula came from what I learned through Spirit World communication in regards to gender and our many lifetimes on Earth. Rula sat quietly while I rambled on with my five minutes of free knowledge before she interjected.

"Mr. Nicholas, are you a New Ager?

I had never been asked that before. I hesitated. "Learning as I go...and you?"

"My girlfriend and I are, too." Rula sighed. "We both believe in doing things that make life easier—like having readings."

"And, that's why I was born a psychic medium–to help you and others." I felt my Mom's presence. Her words echoed through my head. People need to hear what God has to say.

A strong emotional connection to Rula stirred within my empathetic soul. We engaged in a compassionate conversation. I sensed she needed to hear that mediums, too, truly related and understood the generational struggles and backlash to gain ownership of our own unique God-given birthrights.

Rula expressed thanks and appreciation for a remarkable reading and personal insight.

THE VATICAN'S ACCEPTANCE OF PSYCHIC GIFTS

New Age influence of the public's perception of church doctrine finally pushed the Vatican to call for a necessary update, in regards to spiritual gifts, for the highest good and longevity of the Catholic Church.

This long awaited change happened in Vatican City on June 14, 2016 with a summary of the Letter of the Congregation for the Doctrine of the Faith, "Iuvenescit Ecclesia" (The Church rejuvenates), sent out initially to the bishops about the relationship between hierarchical and charismatic gifts. It focused on a summarization of the eight specific topics which follow: (28)

1. Hierarchical and charismatic gifts, co-essential in the life of the Church.

2. Harmonious and complementary connection, with obedience to Pastors.

3. Do not oppose the institutional Church and the Church of charity.

4. May the charismatic dimension never be missing in the Church, but ecclesial maturity is needed.

5. Criteria for discerning authentic charisms.

6. Juridical recognition in accordance with canon law.

7. The relationship between the Universal Church and the particular Churches is essential.

8. Look to the model of Mary.

The Letter, "Iuvenescit," in its entirety, can be viewed at: https://www.vatican.va/roman (25)

An excitement and buzz arose in regards to this new stance on spiritual gifts. For the first time ever, it wholeheartedly welcomed parishioners with the following Charismatic Gifts, known also as Spiritual Gifts: (25)

- The word of wisdom
- The word of knowledge
- Increased faith
- The gift of healing
- The gift of miracles
- The gift of prophecy
- The discernment of spirits
- Diverse kinds of tongues
- Interpretation of tongues

As a devout Catholic and a professional psychic medium myself, this victory resonated deeply within the community of psychics and mediums—as echoed in Anita McMillen's immediate response to the letter.

"I was brought up Catholic, I am still a Catholic," she said. "As a child, I saw and knew things others did not see or know. I have always known this was a gift from God. I remember reading John 12:14 that says, 'He that believeth in me, the works that I do shall he do also; and greater works than these shall he do; because I go unto my Father.' This has been one of my mantras. I was happy to see this article about the Vatican approving spiritual gifts. Many others did not see things as I did and still do, that these gifts were given to myself and others from our Father. Maybe this article will help to clear some of these things up!" (25)

Fenesa Dilworth of the Mandala Soul School Blog commented. "We've all felt the isolation or judgment from the Church, and it has pulled at our hearts because what we do is so beautiful and divinely led. What an opportunity to healing that rift this is. As a lifetime lover of Christ and an equal lover of all faiths, I'm dancing in my living room with this news!" (25)

My thoughts drifted to my great-grandmother, Maria, known as the 'white witch' of Italy, along with Grandma Elizabeth and my mother, Rose, who all took personal vows of secrecy and used precautions when privately exposing their gifts. Each day, if caught, they faced fear of persecution and exile from the Catholic Church and risked severe backlash from the public sector. How truly inhumane, worrisome, and heartbreaking for generations of individuals over the centuries. The Vatican, finally, albeit for its own life and mission of the Church during New Age times, stepped up to the plate to go to bat for total acceptance of all God-given abilities. This good news offered a welcome sigh of relief and a new found gratitude for many—including those in the Spirit World.

"What does this mean for those with Spiritual Gifts?" (25)

• The persecution of those with spiritual gifts, within the context of the Church and its tenants, is over.

• The restriction of spiritual gifts to members of higher-order only has been now released, as they validate that all people can express gifts of the Holy Spirit.

• Lay people, members, in the context of the Church are now encouraged and supported to express their gifts more than ever before in history.

• More and more people are going to feel comfortable coming

forward with their gifts and release their shame of using or having them.

• Spiritual liberation.

Blogger and journalist, Amanda Linette Meder, disseminated the remarkable news about the Vatican update. She asked readers to take a moment to think about the implications of what this meant to them. She offered a toast for liberation to ourselves, our ancestors, and those who have struggled with the oppression of their gifts. Amanda proposed that we all look forward to the future, grateful for all who have prayed for this, both in this lifetime and past ones. (25)

LGBTQ

With the slow growth of New Age acceptance, LGBTQ individuals have put their faith over fear and come out of the closet after decades of hidden shame and secrecy. Born with an inclination to be gay, lesbian, bisexual, transgender, or queer, they joined the movement to be simply loved and accepted as children of God, created in His image.

"2020 statistics revealed that over 63% of Americans reported that homosexuality should be accepted by society. This was a 123% increase from the same report in 2006 which illustrated the rise in acceptance of this community as a whole. An estimated 25.6 million Americans have acknowledged same-sex attractions." (29)

My parents and religious upbringing had taught me that God made us male and female for the sake of marriage and reproduction. When I was a child, initialisms were nonexistent. 'Odd' and 'queer' were the only basic words that I recall. And, to 'old-schoolers' like myself, I didn't hear others until 'gay' and 'homo' increased during the 1960s. It wasn't until around the late 1980s that activists began to use additional terms of distinction to encompass the spectrum of sexuality and gender. (30) Around 2016, the acronym "Q" was reclaimed and added for those who identified as queer or questioning. (29)

With New Age thought, everything has 'come out' in the open including both political and spiritual pushback on various humanitarian issues and rights. On March 15, 2021, the Vatican announced that same-sex marriages could 'not' be blessed by the Church.

"Pope Francis publicly denounced the sacrament of marriage be given to couples other than heterosexual ones. He said, 'God does not and cannot bless sin.' But politically, he claimed that 'the other ones' could be accepted as 'legal unions' outside the church." (30)

GAY PRIESTS: BREAKING THE SILENCE

Weeks after the March 15th public announcement by Pope Francis in regards to the Vatican's refusal to perform marriages for unconventional couples, severe backlash struck on Palm Sunday— March 28, 2021. Jane Pauley hosted *Sunday Morning* with an explosive cover story: "Gay Priests: Breaking the Silence." (31)

That first day of Holy Week, Jane Pauley, opened up a can of worms about the Vatican's awareness of the issue and its habit of sweeping things under the rug to keep it hushed. The segment revealed that an estimated shocking number of homosexual Catholic priests lived secret double-lives within the priesthood. (31)

Reporter Seth Doane conducted a candid conversation to give a voice to an openly gay priest who admitted that the Vatican encouraged them to keep their sexual preferences hidden. CBS dove deep into conversations about the opposition, stigma, and included one with a male sex worker who boasted of having sexual relationships with many of the priests.

And, the review, "Hellish: CBS Profanes Holy Week With Segment on Church Silencing Gay Priests," caught further world attention with its exposure. (31). I did wonder if this segment was in direct response to the Vatican's refusal to budge on its stance in regards to LGBTQ marriages and Church doctrine.

Reporter Seth Doane, interviewed a gay Catholic priest, Father Greg Greitens, from Milwaukee. At age 51, this man of the cloth had 'come out' to his parish. He not only 'got it off his chest' but was welcomed, supported, and understood by congregants who faced similar hurdles in life within their families and friends. Father, a member of the LGBTQ community, disclosed that he respectfully remained celibate—a vow each priest must take but often breaks. According to the Church, it's "acting on" homosexual feelings that makes it a sin. (31) To Father Greg, it was not about sex, but rather finding his own identity and voice.

Unlike Father Greitens, most priests remain anonymous even though they tire of being seen-but-not-heard. If they 'came out,' they risked losing a salary, health care, church housing, pension, and the authority to minister. (31) The assigned church they served may have been the place they grew up in, was baptized, received first Holy Communion, and dedicated a lifetime to God's calling. (31) They wanted to maintain the love, respect, and dignity earned within the church community despite any gay urges they were born with.

Key points from the story included: the Church's need to change its thinking; the Vatican's view of homosexuality as a slow-moving cancer; priest's feelings of being subject to living a double-life or like walking a tightrope; and that the teachings of the church hadn't changed, but the tone was new and important. (31)

A French author, Frédéric Martel, referred to the Vatican as "50 shades of gay" in terms of the prevalence of homosexuality. (31) He stated this population made up the largest silent majority group within the Church. His tell-all book, *In the Closet of the Vatican: Power, Homosexuality, Hypocrisy* became a New York best seller. (31) In it, Francesco Mangiacapra, a sex worker with a law degree, admitted sleeping with hundreds of priests. (31)

175

This zest for humanitarianism in church and and social reform illustrates the basic fundamentals of the New Age Movement in the making.

SEEKING AND SENSING SPIRIT ON SUICIDE

Taking one's own life is a tragic reaction to a stressful experience or nagging thoughts which cause someone to feel unable to cope any longer. Suicide is not the only way to escape one's pain. In addition to counseling, hot lines, or other avenues of help, consider talking with loved ones on the Other Side. After all, suicide affects both realms. Try a psychic medium visit to hear what departed loved ones have to say. Don't be afraid to ask specific questions. The answers may surprise you. Mediums are a wealth of information learned first-hand from spirits. Wipe out the stain of doubt. A candid spiritual perspective can be a real eye-opener.

Katie mustered up the courage to schedule a reading. She never expected to speak with her mother and discover new truths in "A Reason To Live." This particular reading offers hope to anyone faced with similar struggles, or in need of one last ounce of hope and courage.

A Reason to Live

It was the first day of the annual psychic fair at Conneaut Lake Park's historic hotel. Bright sun, jet skis, sail boats, and laughter cheered the air. I set up for my readings in front of a large open window in the lobby overlooking the beach and lake activity.

I organized my table space. The list of names for the day's scheduled readings went directly front and center. Around it, the placement of my usual items: oracle cards, holy water, my mother's pinky finger rosary ring, Dad's silver dollar, Saint Benedict and Archangel Michael medals, a piece of red ribbon, cloves, and other sentimental and meaningful objects.

When I closed my eyes in brief meditation, the clip-clop of sandals grew louder. In that moment, a female spirit connected to me, "She carries heavy pain, mind to toes." Everything stilled. I opened my eyes to my first sitter of the day standing before me. My finger ran across the page to the first name.

"Good morning! I'm Greg. You must be Katie?"

She nodded and gnawed on a fingertip.

"Please sit. We'll get started." An uncontrollable sensation of confusion and despair lurched through my body.

Katie sat slightly slumped in the chair, head dropped. Thick, licorice bangs and curls draped her face. She used her thumbs to simultaneously press down on all ten chewed nails."

That's weird, I thought. "Have you been read before?"

With the hands preoccupied going through the nail rotations, Katie raised her head, shook it sideways and peaked out between bouncy tresses. I wanted to offer her a rubber band or paperclip but moved past my annoyance.

"I need your help, Sir," Katie mumbled. "I don't know what else to do. Someone said you can talk to God."

I fidgeted with objects on my table and nonchalantly added the omitted tissue box.

"Yes, indirectly. Is there anyone in particular that you would like to speak with today?"

Katie's voice strangled to speak. "Just my maker?" She hesitated. "Honestly Sir—I've given up on life. I'll never be accepted or fit in." Her head lowered before she got her last word out.

178

"What makes you feel that way?"

"My Mom disowned me for being gay, and overdosed last year." Tears loosened and bubbled. She made no attempt to wipe them. She closed her eyes and whispered, "Why won't God just take me. I guess He doesn't love or want me either."

I sighed heavily. "Your mother is here with you now. She wants you to know that her love for you has grown strong. She keeps apologizing for the past rejection and hurt."

The girl stiffened upright in the chair. "My Mom? How's that possible? SHE'S DEAD."

"We mediums have the ability to connect you to loved ones who have transitioned into the Spirit World."

Katie blurted, "Can you ask her something?"

"She can hear you. With me as a mouthpiece, I communicate her responses. Now's your chance. Go ahead—let's talk with her."

I noticed the quirky nail rotation begin again. But Katie didn't hesitate to speak up.

"What drug do I need to take to be with you?" Her voice crackled. "Don't let me rot in jail for buyin' crap off the street if it won't do the trick. I just wanna do somethin' right for once."

"Your mother says she is with you everyday—watching over you. She shows me a high roof...some broken bones, cuts, and bruises. She says it wasn't and isn't your time yet."

Katie's teary face twisted. "Why not? Gays don't belong here. Why was I born this way?" Katie grabbed tissues and buried her face into them.

"Oh. Wait," I said. She's explaining the reason...Let me get this straight—"

The wet wad dropped from Katie's clutch. She blankly stared at it, her hands draped limply over her knees.

"Your mother wants you to know it's because you lived before in a dominant role."

Katie's head snapped up. She tucked strands of hair behind the ears.

"It's imprinted within your soul. It carried over. It influences your 'desires.' Embrace it naturally with God's love. Let it not rob you of loving and living life. Stay on the path you are meant to experience."

Katie's eyes grew larger than shooter marbles. Her face glowed. "Really? Wow! Oh my God!" The girl touched my forearm. "Thank you, Sir. I never expected THIS."

I winked. "Your mother's love surrounds you. She's here to help you learn and grow, like she has done herself—in Heaven."

She tapped my wrist. "Can I talk to Mom each time I come back to you?"

"I'm sure she'd like that." More words rushed from my mouth. "You can speak aloud to her everyday. She hears you and sees you. Watch for those beautiful Monarch butterflies she sends."

Katie stood. Her face glowed. She turned to leave but stopped. "Could I please schedule my next reading?"

SALINA'S SONS

A loved one's suicide is never an easy thing to deal with for those left behind. Recovery can be devastating and long-lasting. Such was the case with Salina.

The majority of the time when I'm communicating spiritual messages, a spirit's passing from a suicide starts to come through. As I receive it, I feel a tightness around my neck—a choking sensation. It's my initial sign that someone has either harmed oneself or made an attempt. I wait for the telltale sympathetic signs to hit me: sudden nausea if it was a poisoning; sharp pain in my head, chest, or specific body part if by gunshot....whatever spirit gives me for validation.

I returned from my scheduled lunch break from mediumship appointments one Friday to find a gray-haired woman [Salina] in prayer, seated at my table. Her hands were interlocked with head bowed. When I sat in my chair, she mumbled 'A-A-Amen'. It was obvious during our initial personal introductions that this lady had some sort of speech problem. With her facial tics and tense muscles, she struggled to form sounds and words. I assumed that nervousness or anxiety about getting a reading perhaps made the condition worse than it actually was.

I easily made a connection with the Spirit World. Immediately, my throat felt squeezed. Whenever I feel that way, it is my sign to proceed carefully and cautiously. I have learned over the years that many people may not be ready to hear from 'that' particular beloved one in spirit. But, sometimes, I don't have much choice, if any, in the matter.

A young adult spirit appeared. "I'm sorry!" he said. "Tell my Mom that I'm so sorry. I now see how I took the life from her too when I took my own."

I repeated the son's message. His mother, Salina, sobbed.

A younger male spirit joined him. The two of them stood in silence and stared at each other. I passed that along to my sitter. She cried harder. Through tears and an intermittent stammer, she said that both of them were her sons who recently took their own lives.

At that point, my intermittent sympathetic sensations of being strangled had ended. I took a deep breath.

The youngest spirit spoke. "Please forgive us, Mom."

Their mother shifted in her seat. Her dark eyes penetrated mine. "W-W-Why sh-sh-should I?"

"They ask your forgiveness for their soul progression," I said. "This act of unconditional love holds the past powerless over your life. It allows your heart to find renewed love and connectedness with your boys."

Salina hid her face in her palms and trembled. She subtly wiped away tears on her sleeves.

"Your sons show they are with you at every counseling and speech therapy session."

Her hands fell to her lap, eyes penetrated mine.

"It's 'temporary,' they say. 'We caused it'."

An overwhelming sadness filled me. I could feel Salina's unbearable grief and despair. A mind-flash of the Rx symbol showed pills and needles. I placed the three of them into God's hands in silent prayer.

"Each son says that, at that time, they felt no other option. They selfishly never thought about 'you' or the agony it would create. 'A real hell on earth for you,' they say."

She arched back and nodded. "B-But, I forgive th-them." She humbly made the sign of the cross.

Salina's words seemed to flow a bit smoother.

"Their energy is fading, "I said. "They send lots of love. 'Always at your side, Mom'—they want you to know."

Salina placed her hands on her heart, her fingers splayed out. "I can't thank you 'all' for this message— God truly blessed my prayers. She became suddenly still. "Oh! Did you hear th-that?" A wide smile outlined her yellowed teeth. "I barely st-stuttered!"

She broke into spontaneous laughter mixed with tears and slowly shook her head. "I c-can't believe this!" Reaching across the table, she placed her hand on mine. A warm tingle traveled up my arm.

"Th-thank you Mr. Nicholas," she said. "Thank you!"

Big John, a state policeman, came dressed in uniform to get a reading before he went on duty. He hadn't had a reading in years. At this one, he hoped to communicate with someone who had been on his mind. No further information was given. We began.

I got that tightness in my throat again. A male spirit appeared, dressed exactly like my client. A symbol flashed of a small liquor bottle with an 'X'. I passed that on to my client and asked if he had a fellow officer who may have taken his own life—alcohol related.

"Yes Sir," he said. "In the end, we found his nips stashed everywhere."

"Did you say 'nips'?"

"Yeah, those mini bottles, with about a good shot in each," he said, "that would tide him over 'till he got back to the tavern. Lost his kids, pets, wife, and mind in a rough divorce." He paused and rubbed his bottom lip. He spoke again in a lowered, flat, monotone voice. "Alone, one night, he surrendered his battles; took 'the fifth'— of tequila—with sleeping pills."

"Your buddy shows that he's now sober."

"Like he was in our police academy days?" Big John's chin quivered. His eyes shined with happy tears. "My trusted friend. Better than blood. One of a kind!"

"You always had his back. He still has yours," I said. "'Watching over you,' he says, 'count on him.'"

Big John's face turned rosy. "I'm so glad you're here, Brother. You're missed but never forgotten." He cocked his head to the side. "Until we speak or meet again—it's great to hear from my crime-fighting partner—albeit from the Yonder Side."

BIBLICAL SUPPORT OF MEDIUMS

For four generations, my family never questioned or denied the communication they experienced within the spirit realm. Skepticism reigned only within the public eye. My mother and grandmothers faithfully honored their beliefs and spiritual calling. They knew God had given it to them for His purpose. They each humbly and privately shared their abilities in service and dedication to Him and the Spirit World.

The Paranormal and Supernatural are uniquely mystical. They have no physicality or scientific explanation but rely entirely on pure faith. Believers comprehend that life would be impossible without God's integral powers that surround us. "For nothing will be impossible with God." (Luke 1:37)

"In Him we live and move and have our being." (Acts 17:28) We cannot dictate God's supernatural work in our lives—but only be surprised when it appears.

Skeptics like to quote scripture that indicate a belief in psychic mediums as demonic. Unless the medium is possessed by evil or falseness, I disagree. Not when I've heard spirits relay important messages to a loved one, such as, "I thank you for helping me find religion. I want you to know, Ethel, there is a God!" To me, that's a strong piece of evidence. Would a demon ever say that? I believe that any true phenomena from God always directs us back to Him. Curiosity and participation in His psychic realm will NOT invite evil and devils to one's doorstep to devour souls.

God cautions, but trusts, that we can discern falseness. 1 John 4:1-6 states: "Beloved, do not believe every spirit, but test the spirits to see whether they are from God, for many false prophets have gone out into the world. By this you know the Spirit of God: every spirit that confesses that Jesus Christ has come in the flesh is from God, and every spirit that does not confess Jesus, is not from God. This is the spirit of the Antichrist, which you heard was coming and now is in the world already. Little children, you are from God and have overcome them, for he who is in you is greater than he who is in the world. They are from the world; therefore they speak from the world, and the world listens to them...."

We cannot make or control paranormal and supernatural forces, only God can. He is the creator of the invisible worlds and this visible one. He sent me into this world with Spiritual Gifts and the ability to use my spiritual eyes to see into His invisible component to pass truth, inspiration, and communication between two realms to serve Him and enlighten others.

1 Corinthians 12:7-12 speaks about Spiritualism. "To each is given the manifestation of the Spirit for the common good. For to one is given through the Spirit the utterance of wisdom, and to another the utterance of knowledge according to the same Spirit, to another faith by the same Spirit, to another gifts of healing by the one Spirit, to another the working of miracles, to another prophecy, to another the ability to distinguish between spirits, to another various kinds of tongues, to another the interpretation of tongues. All these are empowered by one and the same Spirit, who apportions to each one individually as He wills...."

God often empowers the Spirit World to interact with people on earth so we may experience godly activity, signs, and messages. As in Revelation 1:1, "The revelation of Jesus Christ, which God gave him to show to his servants the things that must soon take place. He made it known by sending His angel to his servant John."

Jesus said, "Don't be afraid! I am the First and the Last, and the Living One. I was dead, but look—I am alive forever and ever, and I hold the keys to death and Hades." (Revelation 1:17 b-18, HCSB)

"Brothers and sisters, we do not want you to be uninformed about those who sleep in death, so that you don't grieve like the rest of mankind, who have no hope." (1 Thessalonians 4: 13 NIV)

Curiosity has always motivated people to discover what really happens at death and how the paranormal aligns with religion. Most religions or beliefs rely on blind faith as that's all they have. But, Spiritualism is a belief through 'evidential demonstration and validation' as opposed to simply blind faith. It is empowered by a belief in God and created from a divine energy force.

Think about God and prayer. In essence, both fall into the definition of spiritual phenomena. Neither God nor prayer can be proven by any of the sciences, but people wholeheartedly pray and believe. Prayer is a powerful spiritual relationship between the person praying and God. Every time we pray or have one-way conversations with Him, aloud or silently, our loved ones in the Spirit World, obviously hear our prayer requests, thanks, and praises. I believe that Spirit travels through the same door as prayer.

Prayer can produce an observable effect and mediumship can produce evidence using observable spiritual phenomena. Both are spiritual, mystical, and intimate. To me, prayer, mediumship, talking aloud, or with quiet thoughts, are great ways to keep the lines of communication open between us, God, and the Spirit World. It is beneficial for our sense of comfort and well-being.

It's always been second nature for me to accept that through faith alone—God, prayer, and mediums have a Oneness in their connection, parallel to the concept of a Trinity. God is our 'Father.' We pray to Him or His 'Son', Jesus, who was resurrected from the dead. The 'Holy Spirit' gifts His psychic and mediumship abilities to individuals, according to His will.

By faith alone, we naturally accept that we each have a 'soul;' an integral component. Like Him, at deceasement, our spirit, rises from our body and transitions along its journey—for further development and evolution of the 'soul.'

In my profession, mediums hold paranormal powers which means they can go beyond the scope of normal experience and scientific explanation. Spirit-beings are my greatest source of evidential proof of spiritual existence. If we mediums could be coined 'spiritual scientists,' our clarity and preponderance of evidence would more than suffice. How more realistic can Spirits prove themselves to be?

From each reading I do, I continuously learn congruous volumes. Trust me, I deal with spiritual connections everyday. I can see them, hear them, feel them, smell them, sense them, and often taste them, literally. Never doubt that they can't do the same with us! They always prove to me that they divinely know exactly what we recently said, did, thought, felt...or even ate!

I CAN'T BELIEVE WHAT I ATE!

Allow me to share an amusing validation about a young man who came to me for his first spiritual reading. The deceased father immediately came through. All at once, I had a sensation that I was actually chewing something in my mouth.

The spirit waved its arms and shouted. "Tell my son to stop eating my cremated ashes!" I repeated that aloud.

The son's mouth opened and his tongue stretched forward. He grabbed his throat and made choking, gagging sounds.

"Please don't puke," I said. "It's probably been digested and long gone by now."

"NO! NO! I THINK I JUST SWALLOWED THEM ON THE WAY HERE!" He gagged again. "They sure didn't taste like grounds! I bet my dumb wife dumped them into the coffee canister!"

He made a beeline for the bathroom. When he returned, he mentioned that half a cup of his Dad remained in car. He said that he needed to leave due to his upset stomach, re-compose, and figure out what to do about his father's coffee-cremains.

The male-spirit stood with a high energy reserve and another message to relay to his son. "Your Dad says that he's not finished yet."

Instantly, the son slid back into his seat. "What does my father want me to do about this, huh?"

"He shows me a lake, boat, beer, and bungalow. Does that make sense?" I asked.

With a wink and an easy decisive nod, he slowly exhaled.

"Your father giggles. He says he'd rather his ashes be scattered than flushed in a pile of shit!"

We both broke into laughter.

"That's my Dad, alright! I can't believe he's really here...."

SPIRITUAL HISTORY OF SOULS

"History is not the past, it is the present.
We carry our history with us."–James Baldwin

As a psychic medium, it is difficult to discredit the saying that history repeats itself. It often does, especially in regards to the Law of Reincarnation of the human soul—that gives each of us a choice to return to earth if anything remains to be learned and experienced. We are all given the opportunity for numerous do-overs and re-births for the sake of soul progression. Each additional lifetime contributes to the history of a soul.

A North Carolina woman, who had lost both of her children, traveled to PA for her niece's wedding. The bride-to-be, one of my clients, booked her aunt a reading in hopes that this relative could find clarity and comfort. The deceased son came through immediately and offered details about his murder that was made to look like a suicide. When this mother asked to speak to the little sister he said, "She isn't here. She was born again into another family." Reincarnation is often voiced as a truth by the Spirit World.

Some people are returned to earth born as males although their previous lives were female. Others, that were always men, may arrive in female bodies. With historical gender imprints formed by experiences from previous lives, a soul may subconsciously be inclined to have an attraction to the same gender. When a person lives multiple lives as one specific gender in a row, the next incarnation as an opposite one can cause confusion in one's sexual orientation and identity—not to mention conflicts within self, family, friends, society, and religion.

Gender roles tell the story, a history, of a soul's journey and spiritual evolution. Souls sometimes switch roles and genders, as necessary, to learn lessons from previous lives and apply them to the present one. Once we're born, our souls cannot remember a thing. This may be realized, later, through God-given intuition, angels, spirit-beings, soul guides, psychics, mediums, and others... who guide us in goal achievement along our way.

We psychic mediums, along with many minority groups, have experienced injustice for way too long. As we continuously go to bat for any cause, we should never forget our history, for the past can better inform our actions in the present and future. We should never take for granted how others have struggled, fought, or died for our justice, freedom, acceptance, equality, and natural birthrights.

"If you want to understand today, you have to search yesterday."— Pearl Buck

Use history and knowledge to gain clarity and understanding of self and others in order to create positive change in the world, live in greater peace and harmony, with a much needed tolerance and acceptance of everyone's inalienable rights.

Our world is filled with differences in ideas, concepts, cultures, religions, and beliefs. But nobody, but God Himself, holds the real truths of the Universe. Who or what should be judged right or wrong? Why? God loves all of us unconditionally. So, respect the beliefs and opinions of others, be kind, knowledgeable, and try to live life with love and compassion.

Lord Acton famously said, "History is not a burden on the memory but an illumination of the soul."

"History is a symphony of echoes heard and unheard. It is a poem with events as verses."—Charles Angoff

RARE INTERVIEW WITH A PSYCHIC PRIEST

People have stepped out of the boxed walls and confinements of the church doctrine. They have begun to think and explore the truths of existence for themselves.

They seek answers to the paranormal and unknowns via spiritual workshops, palm readers, psychics, mediums, haunted houses, movies, and gallery event demonstrations conducted by authentic presenters, like myself, or the famous Theresa Cuputo, John Edwards...and the like.

Bookstores and libraries offer an increased popularity and selection for spiritual 'food for thought.' I picked up a copy of Allison DuBois's, *We Are Their Heaven*. In it, she conducted a candid interview with a Catholic priest who gracefully balanced his 'Spiritual Gifts' along with a calling from God. It was her opportunity to entertain questions and answers from a very unconventional man of position within the Church. It was uncommon to find a practicing priest who would admit he was a psychic medium let alone discuss it. This interview occurred in the decade prior to the Vatican's update and full acceptance of all mediums. Was Father's advocacy perhaps instrumental to the Church's change in stance?

Allison posed questions on how the priest balanced his collar with being a psychic medium. His replies centered around his beliefs which generally aligned with the Bible.

At one point, she blurted a thought. "People who commit suicide don't go to hell." (32)

She realized what she had said aloud and waited for a negative reaction. The priest responded. "I know, I see them too. I counsel both the living and the dead." (32)

He further clarified that they often seek him out and are in a good place with family and friends. God knew how these victims tried to deal with their own pain. The Church finally changed its stance on suicides and now they're viewed with new understanding.

Further conversation touched on how the church felt about mediums, being created in God's image, and Jesus' resurrection.

Father used Biblical references in support of his responses. "Jesus appeared to people after death...It's in the Bible. This also testifies to the fact that life after death is possible. Not only to exist after your body dies, but for the living to communicate with those who've passed away. Allison, I'm sold on the fact that we're eternal." (32)

He confirmed that the Church acknowledges that mystics truly exist. Its concern was that harmful evils spirits could be brought through by mediums. Allison acknowledged that she had seen more evil in the living but none within the dead.

Mrs. DuBois brought up false prophets. "Father, does the church mean people who pretend to predict or pretend to commune with the dead?" (32)

"Yes," he replied. "People who don't actually have these abilities and are pretending to be a mystic not to help but to harm them." (32)

The priest said that people who aren't what they claim to be are 'false.' But, that didn't translate into authentic mediums or mystics being viewed as bad by the church.

The interview ended with Allison's expressed joy in meeting and sharing conversation over dinner with such a unique man of the cloth who could blend his vocation and spiritual abilities in service of others. She shared her thoughts that 'anybody could be cut from the medium cloth—a mother, a beggar, a child, a priest, anyone.' (32)

As I read the end of Chapter 7, in *We Are Their Heaven*, Allison made a good point that deeply resonated within me. She said, "That as far as religion goes, how is it so different when a medium asks to be believed, in that we can see something that may not be visible to all others? Especially, when you hold a medium's reality next to that of a man of religion who asks people to believe in a God that can't be seen? It's not so different. Both claims center around one's belief and personal experiences. Both are leaps of faith. Often faiths overlap, as they should, because both focus on something bigger than the living." (32)

I vicariously internalized and identified with the like-mindedness of the priest and Mrs. DuBois. The compatibility in their beliefs and experiences, in comparison to my own, reflected evident truths. And, to me, being a devout Catholic alongside of a practicing psychic medium, the two entities always blended naturally, rightfully, and faithfully in God's honor.

SEEDS OF AWARENESS

My mother's teachings had always reinforced the existence of major differences between Old Testament and New Testament to be considered for thought. Even though religion was built on their foundations and truths, they were open for evaluation and correction as God's revelations continued to unfold and become obvious. God and His Creation are not stagnant, but living and constantly evolving which creates necessary change within us and the world in which we live. We indeed have witnessed several transformations in the Church, and trust that more will follow, as God's love leads us to our highest good in His ongoing plans for the Universe.

A passage of (2 Timothy 3:16-17) speaks volumes. It says that "all Scripture is breathed out by God and profitable for teaching, for reproof, for correction, and for training in righteousness, that the man of God may be competent, equipped for every good work."

During a medium reading with a client, a female spirit vividly showed a double weigh scale. With palms up, she made a point of showing how the scales hung with 'what we were taught' on one hand and 'what we know now,' on the other. Spirit mentioned the weight had begun to shift and tip toward increased awareness of the Spirit World. She showed a small stack of books and noted that more information needed to be written and published to plant more seeds of awareness—which inspired *Old World Psychic Medium: Gregory Nicholas*. I wrote this book, not as the psychic medium I was meant to be, but also as the spiritually awakened man that I've become.

SPIRITUALIST

Sensitive people all around

Prove the Harmony that can abound

Is present in all

Right here and now

Interested in others insistent on truth

Through Faith and Love and those above

Using our thoughts and Hearts

Accepting our test's and task's

Living each day to it's fullest

Inspired by all that's near

Steadily walking life's path

Today Tomorrow and Forever

> Members of the Adult Unfoldment Class
> First Spiritualist Church-Brockton
> Rev. Gertrude Stevens, Pastor

"The bridge which crosses the stream of Death should have six planks–they are faith, hope, charity, forgiveness, kindness, and humility." —Sir Arthur Conan Doyle

REFERENCES

1. **theconversation.com.** The 'Christmas Star' apperas again: Jupiter and Satrun align in the 'great conjunction' on Dec. 21, 2020. *The Conversation.* [Online] 12 22, 2020. [Cited: 12 27, 2020.] https://theconversation.com/the-christmas-star-appears-again-jupiter-and-saturn-align-in-the-great-conjunction-on-dec-21-2020-152370.

2. **mypandit.com.** Impact of Mercury, Jupiter, Saturn Conjunction. *mypandit.com.* [Online] 01 02, 2021. [Cited: 01 05, 2021.] http://www.mypandit.com/article/triple-conjunction-jupiter-mercury-satrun-in-capricorn.

3. **Heasley, Karen and Linville, Susan Urbanek.** *Treasures from the Spirit World.* New Castle : Pokeberry Press, 2018. pp. 55-81.

4. **National Spiritualist Association of Churches.** *Spiritual Manual.* s.l. : National Spiritualist Association of Churches, 2002. p. 32. Vols. Revision of August, 2002.

5. **Francis, Pope.** Guradian Angel Prayer. *Daily Bread.* [Online] 11 05, 2020. https://www.catholicfaithstore.com/daily-bread/guardian-angel-prayer.

6. **Wikipedia.** Dominoes. *Wikipedia.* [Online] 06 26, 2020. [Cited: 07 29, 2021.] https://en.wikipedia.org/wiki/Dominoes.

7. —. Divination. *Widipedia.* [Online] https://en.wikipedia.org/wiki/Divination.

8. **Vedantu.** White LIght. *Vednatu.com.* [Online] [Cited: 04 06, 2021.] https://www.vedantu.com/physics/white-light.

9. **History.com Editors.** Ether and Chloroform. *History.* [Online] 08 21, 2018. [Cited: 06 32, 2020.] https://www.history.com/topics/inventions/ether-and-chloroform.

10. **HiggyPop.** Why Is Veil Between The Worlds Thinner At Halloween. *HiggyPop.* [Online] 10 04, 2019. [Cited: 10 29, 2020.] https://www.higgypop.com/news/why-is-veil-between-the-worlds-thinner-at-halloween.

11. **Wikipedia.** List of natural phenomena. *Wikipedia.* [Online] 10 05, 2021. [Cited: 06 21, 2021.] https://en.wikipedia.org/wiki/List_of_ natural_phenomena.

12. **Hoy, Tana.** Psychic Phenomenon Science. *Tanahoy.com.* [Online] 12 30, 2016. [Cited: 09 01, 2021.] https://www.tanahoy.com/psychic-phenomenn-science/.

13. **Marquis, Natalie Eve.** Free Visual Guide to the 8 Clair Senses. *Natalie Marquis.* [Online] 01 30, 2016. [Cited: 06 20, 2020.] http:// nataliemarquis.com/free-visual-guide-to-the-8-clair-senses/.

14. **Keen Editorial Staff.** Psychic, Intuitive, Medium: What's the Difference? *keen.* [Online] [Cited: 07 30, 2020.] https://www.keen.com/ articles/psychic/psychic-intuitive-medium-whats-the-difference.

15. **Richardson, Tanya Carroll.** A Professional Psychic On How To Develop The 4 'Clairs' Of Intuition. *mbgmindfulness.* [Online] 03 02, 2021. [Cited: 07 30, 2021.] https://www.mindbodygreen.com/articles/ the-4-types-of-intuition-and-how-to-tap-into-each.

16. **Pavlina, Erin.** What are the four clairs of psychic ability? *Erin Pavlina.* [Online] 08 01, 2011. [Cited: 07 30, 2021.] https://www. erinpavlina.com/blog/2011/08/what-are-the-four-clairs-of-psychic-ability/.

17. **Wikipedia.** List of pyschic abilities. *Wikipedia.* [Online] 10 31, 2021. [Cited: 02 10, 2121.] https://en.wikipedia.org/wiki/List_of_psychic_ abilities.

18. —. Age of Aquarius. *Widipedia.* [Online] 09 30, 2021. [Cited: 03 04, 2021.] https://en.wikipedia.org/wiki/Age_of_Aquarius.

19. **Fox, Jan.** The Age of Pisces is ending, the Age of Aquarius is Dawning! What to expect. *Astrolada.* [Online] 09 23, 2012. [Cited: 04 24, 2021.] https://www.astrolada.com/articles/predictive-astrology/the-age-is-pisces-is-ending-the-age-of-aquarius-is-dawning-what-to-expect. html.

20. **Martinez, Melissa.** Aquarius Zodia Sign Guide! *Aquarius Sign Dates, Traits, & More.* [Online] 06 19, 2011. [Cited: 07 31, 21.] https:// www.insightfulpsychics.com/aquarius-zodiac-sign-guide/.

21. **Fox, Jan.** The Age of Pisces - The Age of Deception. *wake up world.* [Online] 09 23, 2012. [Cited: 07 30, 2021.] https://wakeup-world.com/2012/09/24/the-age-of-pisces-the-age-of-deception/.

22. **Hayes, Lynn.** Astrological Musings: Androgyny and the Aquarian Age. *beliefnet.* [Online] 07 01, 2011. [Cited: 12 18, 2021.] https://www.beliefnet.com/columnists/astrologicalmusings/2011/07/androgyny-and-the-aquarian-age.html.

23. **Astrology Answers.** Astrology Term Dictionary. *New Age.* [Online] [Cited: 05 16, 2021.] https://astrologyanswers.com/astrology_definitions/n/new-age/.

24. **Dunn, Lily.** What is the New Age Movement? *exploreGod.* [Online] [Cited: 07 20, 2021.] https://www.exploregod.com/articles/what-is-the-new-age-movement.

25. **Meder, Amanda Linette.** Vatican Update: The ChurchApproves of Psychic Gifts. *Amanda Linette Meder.* [Online] 04 02, 2017. [Cited: 04 15, 2021.] https://www.amandalinettemeder.com/blog/vatican-now-approves-of-spiritual-gifts-heres-what-this-means-for-lay-people.

26. **Anderson, Alan C. and Whitehouse, Deborah G.** New Age and the New Thought Movement. *ppquimby.com.* [Online] 06 21, 1997. [Cited: 05 15, 2021.] https://ppquimby.com/alan/newage.htm.

27. **All About GOD Ministries.** New Age. *All About Spirituality.* [Online] [Cited: 03 20, 2021.] https://www.allaboutspirituality.org/new-age.htm.

28. **Holy See Press Office.** Summary of the Letter "iuvenescit Ecclesia" (The Church rejuvinates), 14.06.2016. *Summary of Bulletin.* [Online] 06 14, 2016. [Cited: 07 08, 2021.] https://press.vatican.va/content/salastampa/en/bollettino/pubblico/2016/06/14/160614a.html.

29. **Iovannone, Jeffrey J.** A Brief History of the LGBTQ Initialism. *Medium.com.* [Online] 05 30, 2019. [Cited: 03 20, 2021.] https://medium.com/queer-history-for-the-people/a-brief-history-of-the-lgbtq-initialism-e89db1cf06e3.

30. **Ring, Trudy.** Catholic Church 'Cannot Bless Sin,' Pope Says of Same-Sex Unions. *Advocate.* [Online] 03 15, 2021. [Cited: 03 30, 2021.] https://www.advocate.com/religion/2021/3/15/catholic-church-cannot-bless-sin-pope-says-same-sex-unions.

31. **Hays, Gabriel.** HELLISH: CBS Profanes Holy Week With Segment on Church Silencing Gay Preists. *mrcNewBusters.* [Online] 03 30, 2021. [Cited: 03 30, 2021.] https://www.newsbusters.org/blogs/culture/gabriel-hays/2021/03/30/hellish-cbs-profanes-holy-week-segment-church-silencing-gay.

32. **DuBois, Allison.** *We Are Their Heaven: Why the Dead Never Leave Us Behind.* New York : Simon & Shuster, 2006. pp. 196-202.

CONTACT INFORMATION

Email: psychicgregnick@yahoo.com

Like / Follow Greg Nicholas on Facebook